PAM BONO DESIGNS

Quilt It For Kids

11 Quilt Projects • Sports, Fantasy & Animal Themes
Quilts for Children of All Ages

C&T PUBLISHING

Editor: Liz Aneloski
Technical Editor: Carolyn Aune
Copy Editor: Vera Tobin
Cover Designer: Kristen Yenche
Book Designer: Rose Sheifer/Graphic Productions
Design Director: Kathy Lee
Illustrator: Pam Bono
Photographer: Sharon Risedorph
Front Cover: That's My Baby (detail)
Back Cover: Carousel

Published by C&T Publishing, Inc., P.O. Box 1456,
Lafayette, California 94549

Thank you to Mr. and Mrs. Brian Evans for opening their home
for the photographs on pages 16, 50, 78, 95, 103

Thank you to Shapell Industries for allowing the photography
in their model homes at the Bridges at Gate Ranch in San
Ramon, CA.

Attention Teachers:
C&T Publishing, Inc. encourages you to use this book as a text for teaching. Contact us at 800-284-1114 or www.ctpub.com for more information
about the C&T Teachers Program.

Library of Congress Cataloging-in-Publication Data

Quilt it for kids : 11 quilt projects : sports, fantasy & animal
themes for children of all ages / Pam Bono Designs.
          p. cm.
Includes bibliographical references and index.
     ISBN 1-57120-090-8 (pbk.)
  1. Patchwork. 2. Machine sewing. I. Pam Bono Designs (Firm)
     TT835 .B627 2000
     746.46'041—dc21

                              99-6826
                               CIP

Printed in Hong Kong
10 9 8 7 6 5 4 3 2 1

Contents

Dedication

This book is dedicated to the memory of the dearest friend of our lives, Dorothy Ismay Davis of Durango, Colorado. You are with us always, and your strength and unconditional love gave us everything we needed to continue with our work. Your love of Durango is a part of our souls forever, and allowing us to fulfill our Hopalong Cassidy fantasies is an everlasting memory. We all miss you.

Special thanks to:

- Our tenor/artist/writer son Dallas for his wonderful, humorous contributions to this book. You give all of us the ability to laugh at ourselves once in a while.

- Our computer guru son Ryan and his wife Cheryl Renee. Ryan, thanks for always being there to fix sick computers and printers—even over the phone. To Cheryl, special love for entering our life with your beauty, joyful outlook, and for truly being our daughter.

- Our Canadian design partner and dear friend, Mindy Kettner, for her continuous support and contributing amazing designs along with her quick wit. We love you.

- Sylvia Gauthier and Terri Lightman of The Crafty Quilter in Cody, Wyoming, for last-minute help with binding the quilts.

- Our new friend and marketing manager, Nikki Pottier. We wouldn't be doing all that we are doing without you. Your creative ideas and loving personality are a treasure. Thanks for coming into our lives, along with your "big bear."

- All of the staff at C&T who have worked so hard with us to make this book a success. Special thanks to Todd Hensley, Trish Katz, and Liz Aneloski for your patience, dedication, and understanding.

- Faye Gooden and Suzanne Gamble of Suzanne's Sewing in Durango, Colorado. Faye, your quilting creations are exquisite and have enhanced our work beautifully. Thanks to Suzanne for your friendship and beautiful work.

- Wanda Nelson of Farmington, New Mexico for your beautiful quilting and for being our friend.

- P&B Textiles and Benartex Textiles for their contributions of fabric.

- Special thanks to Bernina Of America for their terrific machines, and to New Home Sewing Machines for our amazing Janome 9000.

Introduction

This is not a book on "How to Quilt," "Quick Piecing Techniques for Beginners," or "Quilts to Make in a Weekend." When we began this book, our ultimate goal was to produce a variety of designs to be enjoyed by all quilters, regardless of age. There are many books available which are great teaching devices for quilting (see Bibliography, page 110). We suggest that beginners study the rotary cutting techniques, patchwork basics, and quilting techniques given in those books before you begin the projects in this one.

Concise, illustrated instructions for the techniques used in this book begin on page 8. Reading these instructions, reviewing the illustrations, and practicing a bit will help speed you through the projects. Some of the quilt tops can be made in a weekend and are easy for beginners, while others take longer, but the effort you put into any of the projects will yield great rewards.

This is a book about making something to be treasured for generations and putting an everlasting smile on the face of a beloved child in your life. You can personalize many of the designs with the memories, names, and events of childhood. Some will even become cherished quilts for the child inside every adult.

This book has special meaning for us because it is the brainchild of four people; including our son Dallas and our wonderful design partner Mindy. We wanted to address as many different interests as we could for children of all ages, adding some humor along the way. Dallas's off-the-wall sense of humor and Mindy's bright outlook and quick wit come alive in all of their designs.

We hope you enjoy the projects as much as we enjoyed creating them.

Happy Quilting.
Pam and Robert Bono

How to Use This Book

We have given you as many visual tools as possible, but reading the instructions often alleviates a lot of frustration. The following tips will help you understand how everything has been presented.

The lists of materials indicate what you need to make each quilt as shown. Select similar fabrics, or substitute fabrics in the colors of your choice. Fabric selection tips appear at the beginning of each project. A color key is given for each fabric, so you can match each fabric with the accompanying color-coded illustrations. We recommend 100% cotton fabric for quilt tops and backing. Wash, dry, and press fabrics before cutting.

These quilts were designed and made in 1999. Remember that fabric manufacturers change their fabric lines about every six months; therefore if you are looking for the exact fabrics you see in the photos, you are unlikely to find a perfect match. In our fabric tips, we may suggest (for example) a "grass" fabric. Your chances of finding something similar to what we used may be very good, so don't give up! Catalogs and the Internet are good places to look if your quilt or fabric shop does not have just what you want.

Yardages are based on 45"-wide fabric, allowing for up to 4% shrinkage unless otherwise specified. Our cutting instructions are generally based on 42" wide strips, to allow for shrinkage and trimming of selvages. Trim your selvage with the least possible loss as some of the cuts may require a $42\frac{1}{4}$" width.

All seam allowances are $\frac{1}{4}$" and are included in all stated measurements and cutting instructions. We have tested the cutting instructions when making our quilts, trying for the least waste. Most scraps are used. Please read instructions for the project before you begin to cut. This can eliminate many errors.

Cutting instructions are for the whole quilt as shown. If you want to make just one block, see How to Make One Block (page 13).

Cut everything in the order given. Large pieces such as sashings and borders are generally cut first to be sure you have enough fabric. There are cutting instructions for each fabric; the first cuts are generally a specified number of cross-grain (selvage to selvage) strips. Second cuts are indented. These instructions specify how to cut the strips into smaller pieces.

The identification of each piece follows in parentheses, consisting of the block letter and unit number that correspond to the illustrations. The pieces shown in the assembly diagrams are "units," such as A1 or A1a. A refers to the Block letter and 1 or 1a refers to the unit.

Many cut pieces may be used in more than one unit. In this case, several unit numbers may be given in the parentheses.

Organize cut pieces in zip-top bags, and label each bag (using masking tape) with the appropriate unit numbers, even if the piece has several unit numbers. This not only avoids confusion and cut pieces lying all over the place, but it keeps the pieces stored safely until you need them. We generally organize our work by putting all bags of like fabric together so we don't have to hunt for a specific color.

Read and practice all of the quick piecing techniques used in the book if you are not accustomed to them. Practice makes perfect! Cutting and piecing instructions are in a logical step-by-step progression. Follow this order to avoid confusion. Although a picture is worth a thousand words (and we have given you many pictures), please read the instructions and refer to the illustrations often.

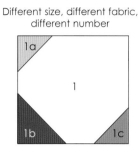

Strip-set illustrations show the size of the segments to be cut from that strip set. Keep the strip-set units in zip-top plastic bags and label them as you have the other units.

Every project has one or more block designs. Instructions include block illustrations that show the fabric colors and the numbered units that correspond to the numbered units in the cutting list. It is important that you read the instructions as you look at the block diagram so you assemble the block in the correct order. Individual units are assembled first, using one or more of the quick-piecing techniques described in the Techniques section beginning on page 8.

Some blocks and many units have mirror images. For easy reference, we've included illustrations for both blocks. Refer to these illustrations often.

Each unit in the assembly diagram is numbered. The main part of the unit is indicated with the number only. A diagonal line and color change represents a seam where a diagonal corner or end is attached. Each diagonal piece is numbered with the main unit number plus a letter (such as 1a).

Unit Numbering

Some units have multiple diagonal corners or ends. When these are the same size and are cut from the same fabric, the identifying letter is the same.

Same size, same fabric, same number

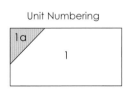

If the unit has multiple diagonal pieces that are different in size and/or color, the letters are different. These pieces are always joined to the main unit in alphabetical order.

Different size, different fabric, different number

Triangle-squares are shown as assembled, with the unit number in the center of the square.

Unit number in center

Follow the unit identification system carefully as you piece each block. Organizing your work as suggested will save time and avoid confusion.

Piecing instructions are given for making one block. Even if the quilt requires ten of the same block, the instructions are given for one block only. You will be instructed as to how many blocks to make to complete the project as shown.

The quilts in this book can be made in a reasonable amount of time because of the methods used. Using The Angler 2™ will speed things along considerably, but remember that everyone works at his or her own pace. Don't feel you are running a race with the clock to complete your project—it's such fun to see the block take shape as you go. Remember, creating something from nothing is very satisfying. Relax and enjoy!

Techniques

The techniques in this book may be accomplished by following the instructions below. We have also included graphics and instructions for the use of The Angler 2™, a piecing tool designed by Robert Bono. This tool is not a prerequisite for completing any of the projects, but is strongly recommended, since it cuts piecing time in half for many of the techniques. This new upgrade of the original Angler™ aids in making squares as large as 7¾".

Traditional Sewing

Strip Piecing

Some of the projects in this book require you to join strips of different fabrics to make what is called a strip set. The instructions and graphics given with these projects specify how to cut strips and give precise measurements for cutting segments.

To make a strip set, match each pair of strips with right sides together. Stitch through both layers along one edge. Keeping raw edges matched is of utmost importance as is maintaining an accurate ¼" seam.

To keep your strip sets straight when you're stitching multiple strips in a set, we suggest that you use "anti-directional" stitching. When you add a new strip, sew each new seam in the *opposite* direction from the last one.

Anti-directional Stitching

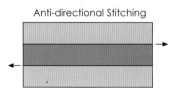

This helps to distribute tension evenly in both directions, and keeps the strip set from getting warped and wobbly. You should press all seams towards the darkest color fabric.

After cutting, assembling, and pressing your strip set, you will be directed to cut it into segments that fit into the design as "units." Use a ruler to measure, then make appropriate crosswise cuts for individual segments. This technique is fast and accurate since you assemble and press each unit before it is cut from the strip set.

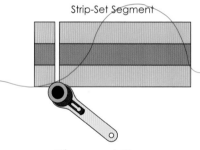

Strip-Set Segment

Diagonal Corners

This technique turns squares into sewn triangles. It is especially helpful if the corner triangle is very small and would be hard to handle. The little pieces we were once afraid to piece become a snap when we use this technique.

There is no guesswork involved in determining where seam allowances meet when you sew squares to squares or squares to rectangles. The ease and speed with which you'll sew these corners will amaze you, and chain piecing is a natural for larger numbers of diagonal corners.

All project instructions will give the size of the fabric pieces required for

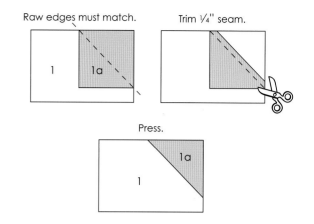

the design. The base piece can be either a square or a rectangle; however, the contrasting corner is always a square.

Draw or press a seam guide line from corner to corner on each diagonal corner square. We suggest using a fine-tipped marker since a pencil tends to drag and distort the fabric, leaving room for error. After time and practice, you should be able to stitch small squares (up to 1½") by eye without having to mark a seam guide line.

With right sides together, match the small square to the appropriate corner of the base fabric. It is very important that the raw edges stay well aligned—do not let them shift. Stitch from corner to corner.

Raw edges must match.

After the corner square is stitched, trim the seam to ¼" on the diagonal square fabric only. Keeping the base fabric intact gives stability and aids in accuracy.

Trim ¼" seam.

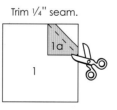

Press the triangle open so the pieced corner covers the corner of the base fabric.

Press.

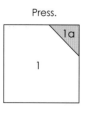

Many of the designs will call for a double diagonal corner. This need not be confusing if corners are always added in alphabetical order. Join, trim, and press the first diagonal corner as above.

Raw edges must match. Trim ¼" seam.

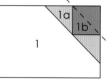

Press.

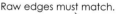

Then add the second, smaller diagonal corner over the first. Trim seam and press.

Raw edges must match.

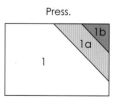

Trim ¼" seam.

Press.

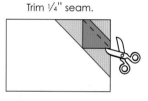

When making large diagonal corners, which are used in many of the designs in this book, it is essential to keep raw edges matched. In this case we suggest pinning the raw outside edges to keep the large corner square from shifting when it is sewn.

Pin raw edges.

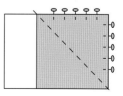

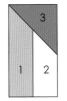

To add a diagonal corner to a strip set, follow the instructions on page 9 to mark, stitch, trim, and press.

Add a diagonal corner to a strip set.

Diagonal Ends

This method is similar to the diagonal-corner technique, but it joins two rectangles on the diagonal. Project instructions will specify the size of each rectangle. This technique is also used to make continuous binding strips.

To stitch diagonal ends, position the top rectangle so it is perpendicualr to the base rectangle, right sides together. Again, proper alignment of raw edges is critical. Mark a diagonal line across the end of the top rectangle in the same manner as for diagonal corners, beginning in the corner where the two fabrics meet and angling upward to the opposite corner of the base rectangle at a 45° angle. Stitch on the marked line.

Diagonal End, Left Slant   Diagonal End, Right Slant

Trim away the excess fabric from the corner seam allowance.

Diagonal End, Left Slant   Diagonal End, Right Slant

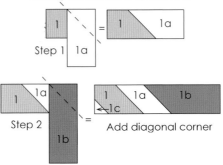

Making continuous diagonal ends

When diagonal ends need to be made in mirror image sets, be careful to draw your sewing line in the correct direction.

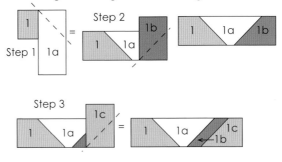

Making mirror image continuous diagonal ends

Please note that some diagonal end units will also include an added diagonal corner. In this case, diagonal ends are made first; then diagonal corners are to added to complete the unit.

Triangle-Squares

Although the grid method of making triangle-squares is useful for making many squares at once, we do not use it frequently since the projects in this book do not call for large numbers of triangle-squares. We have also found that drawing grids tends to distort the fabric, and completed squares do not always end up the same size. By making one or two traingle-squares at a time according to the illustrations shown, you will be more consistently accurate. You can easily chain piece these triangle-squares in the same amount of time that it takes to draw grids.

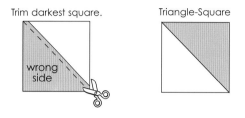

To make two triangle-squares, mark a seam guide line diagonally through the center of the square on the wrong side of the lightest fabric. Place the two fabrics right sides together, then stitch an accurate ¼" seam on each side of the center line. Using your rotary cutter, cut through both squares, between the stitching along the drawn center line. This will yield two triangle-squares.

Mark, stitch, and cut.

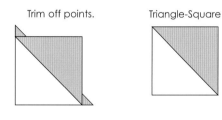

Press seams toward the darkest fabric and trim off the points.

Trim off points.   Triangle-Square

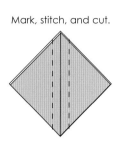

In some of the designs you may be directed to make one triangle-square. To do so, mark your seam guide line diagonally through the center of the square on the wrong side of the lightest fabric. Place the two fabrics right sides together, and stitch on the drawn line.

Mark and stitch.

Trim the darkest fabric only, leaving a ¼" seam allowance, and press the triangle-square open. We frequently use this method when we only need one triangle-square. Although this method uses a bit more fabric, it is quick and extremely accurate.

Trim darkest square.   Triangle-Square

wrong side

Robert's Special Appliqué Technique

The technique Robert developed is a quicker way to create fusible appliqué because the appliqué shapes are not drawn on the appliqué film (the appliqué shapes are rotary cut). Although this method uses a bit more appliqué film, we found the time it saved was invaluable.

For Robert's "quick appliqué placement" method, you will need either notebook paper or laser printer paper. Newspaper will not work, nor will any other paper with printing on it, since the printing could transfer to the fabric.

Lay a piece of plain paper on your ironing board or pad. Place the rotary-cut appliqué shape wrong side up on the paper; then cut a piece of appliqué film (such as Wonder Under®) a bit larger than the appliqué fabric, but smaller than the paper. Place the appliqué film on top of the appliqué fabric with the adhesive side of the film on the wrong side of the fabric. Be sure the appliqué film is smaller than your piece of paper or you will end up with appliqué film all over your ironing board!

Press following the manufacturer's instructions. If the appliqué is larger than the surface of the iron, you will need to move the iron on top of the appliqué film until all areas of the appliqué film have been fused.

Using sharp scissors, or your rotary cutter if the piece has straight edges, cut around the outside edges of the appliqué. The paper will fall away, and you should be able to peel the appliqué film away easily. Your appliqué piece is now ready to be pressed into place on the fabric background. With this method, smaller appliqué pieces may be placed side by side to cover up most of the paper, and there's no more drawing or tracing! It works great!

Two French-Fold Binding Techniques

The best binding for quilts is a double-layer binding frequently called French-fold binding. Double-layer binding wears well and is easy to make and apply. Straight-grain binding is best for quilts with straight sides. Make bias binding only when your quilt is an irregular shape or has rounded corners. A walking foot is helpful for sewing binding to the quilt.

Each project specifies the number of strips to cut for straight or bias binding. Cut 2 1/2" wide, these strips result in finished binding that is approximately 1/2" wide. You may wish to make wider binding for quilts with thick batting.

Use the diagonal-end technique (page 10) to join two strips end to end. Make continuous binding from all of the strips called for in the project you are making. Trim seam allowances to 1/4" and press seams open.

Join strips together end to end.

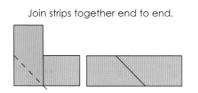

Technique 1
Mitered Corners

With wrong sides together, press the binding in half along the length of the strip. With raw edges aligned, place the binding on the front of the quilt top, in the middle of any

side. Leave a 3" tail of binding free before the point where you begin stitching.

Place a pin 1/4" from the corner of the quilt. Using an accurate 1/4" seam, stitch through all layers. Stop stitching at the pin and backstitch. Remove the quilt from the machine and cut the threads.

Stop stitching 1/4" from corner.

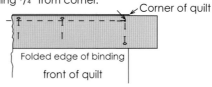

Rotate the quilt 1/4 turn. Fold the binding straight up, away from the corner, and make a 45° diagonal fold.

Fold binding.

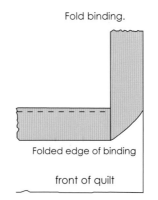

Bring the binding straight down so it is even with the quilt edge, leaving the top fold even with the raw edge of the previously sewn side. Begin stitching at the top edge, sewing through all layers.

Fold binding and stitch.

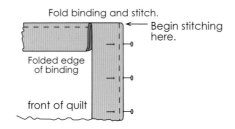

Stitch all corners in this manner.

Stop stitching as you approach the beginning point. Fold the 3" tail of binding over on itself and pin in place. The end of the binding will overlap this folded section. Continue stitching through all layers to 1" beyond the folded tail. Trim the end of the binding.

Trim the batting and backing nearly even with the seam allowance, leaving a bit extra to fill the binding.

Fold the binding over the seam allowance to the back. When turned, the beginning fold conceals the raw end of the binding. Slipstitch the folded edge of the binding to the backing fabric. Fold a miter into the binding at back corners.

Fold binding to back and slipstitch.

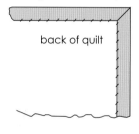

back of quilt

Technique 2
Square Corners

Prepare binding as for mitered-corner binding. With raw edges aligned, place the binding along one side edge of the front of the quilt from corner to corner. Machine stitch the binding to that edge and trim the excess binding at ends. Repeat for the opposite side edge of the quilt. Turn the binding over the raw edge, and use matching thread to slipstitch the binding on the quilt back.

To bind the top edge of the quilt, begin at the top left corner. Match the raw edges of the binding and quilt and wrap 1" of the binding around the corner to the back side of the quilt.

Wrap 1" of binding to back side of quilt.

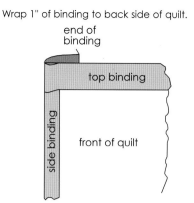

end of binding

top binding

side binding

front of quilt

Pin in place. Pin the binding all the way across the top edge of the quilt front. Trim the excess binding, leaving 1" to wrap around the corner to the back. Stitch the binding to the top edge of the quilt through all thicknesses, including the 1" corner wrap. Fold the binding over to the back side. This will encase the raw edges at the corners. Slipstitch the binding to the backing. Repeat for the bottom edge of the quilt.

How to Make One Block

The cutting instructions are for the quilt as it is shown in the photograph. If you want to make only one block for your own special creation, follow the instructions given below.

● Each cutting list and each project is accompanied by an illustration of the block(s). The unit numbers in the cutting list correspond to the units in the block illustrations. Count how many of each unit are in the block illustration. Instead of cutting the number shown in the cutting list, cut the number you need for one block.

● If you prefer, you can figure it out from the cutting list alone. If the quilt shown has ten blocks, for example, then divide each quantity by ten to determine how many pieces you need for one block.

Sewing with The Angler 2™

Diagonal Corners

Line up diagonal corners, raw edges matching, as in the diagonal corner instructions (page 9). The right side of the square should be aligned with the first 45° diagonal line on the right as shown. The tip of the fabric will fall under the needle. You will not need to draw seam guide lines unless the square is larger than 7¾".

Line up fabric with first 45° line.

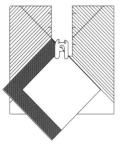

As the feed dogs pull the fabric through the machine, keep the fabric aligned with the diagonal lines on the right until you can see the center line at the bottom of The Angler 2. Keep the tip of the square on this line as the diagonal corner is fed through the machine. Trim the seam and press.

Keep tip of square on center line of Angler.

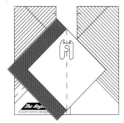

Diagonal Ends

Refer to illustrations for making diagonal ends (page 10) for right-slant and left-slant.

Align top rectangle with the first 45° diagonal line on the right side of The Angler 2. Align the bottom rectangle with the first 45° left line as shown.

Line fabric up with first 45° line.

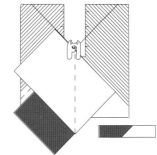

As the feed dogs pull the fabric through the machine, keep the fabric aligned with the diagonal lines on the right until you can see the center line at the bottom of The Angler 2. Keep the top of the rectangle on this line as it is fed through machine as shown.
Trim seam and press.

Keep tip of square on center line of Angler 2.

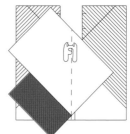

For left slant, align the top rectangle with the first 45° diagonal line on the left side of The Angler 2 as shown.

Align fabric with first 45° line.

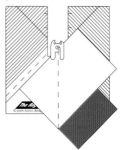

As the rectangles are fed through the machine, keep the top rectangle aligned with the left diagonal lines on The Angler 2 until you can see the center bottom line. Trim seam and press.

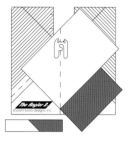

Turn the square around and repeat for the other seam. Seams will be ¼" from center as shown.

Cut triangle-squares apart on center line. Trim off tips and press.

Triangle-Squares

For triangle-squares, refer to the Triangle-Square instructions on pages 10-11. Align the right side of the squares with line 1 on the right side of The Angler 2 as shown. Align the left side of the square with the dashed diagonal line on The Angler 2.

Line up fabric with line 1 on the right and the second diagonal line on the left.

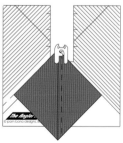

As the feed dogs pull the square through the machine, keep the top part of the square aligned with the diagonal lines on the The Angler 2 until the left seam line is visible. Keep the point on this line until the seam is sewn.

Accurate ¼" Seam Allowance

Allign pieced units on Angler 2 as shown for an accurate ¼" seam allowance.

Seam line alignment.

FABRIC TIPS ▶ Soft colors combined with beautiful trim and ribbon roses make this quilt a dancer's dream. The 3-D tutu and sleeves are sewn using a fine, white netting, giving our ballerina the appearance of a dancer in the clouds. Pale pink enhances the appliqué toe shoe on the pocket, which is the perfect place to store your little ballerina's own special shoes.

Materials

■ Fabric I	(dark blue print)	1 yard
■ Fabric II	(dark pink print)	¼ yard
■ Fabric III	(dark pink solid)	⅛ yard
■ Fabric IV	(light pink print)	⅜ yard
☐ Fabric V	(white-on-white print)	¾ yard
■ Fabric VI	(light blue print)	¼ yard
■ Fabric VII	(solid flesh)	¼ yard
■ Fabric VIII	(solid black)	⅛ yard
Backing		1⅜ yards
Batting		37" x 48"
Fine white netting (48" wide)		½ yard
¼"-wide pink ribbon		3 yards
1⅜"-wide fancy white lace trim		⅝ yard
¾"-wide white heart lace trim		⅜ yard
⅛"-wide string pearls		¼ yard
½" blue ribbon roses		6
Appliqué film		large scrap
Red, blue, and black fine-tipped fabric pens		

Cutting

■ *From Fabric I, cut: (dark blue print)*

- One 11½"-wide strip. From this, cut:
  - One - 2¼" x 11½" (Spacer 43)
  - One - 2" x 11½" (B4)
  - One - 7⅝" x 10⅞" (A39)
  - One - 6⅛" x 10⅞" (A38)
  - One - 2" x 9⅜" (A34)
  - One - 7¼" x 8" (A15)
  - One - 2" x 8" (A14)
  - One - 4¼" x 7½" (Spacer 41)
  - One - 5" x 7¼" (A33)
  - One - 3½" x 7¼" (A29)

- From scrap, cut:
  - Four - 2" squares (A9, A13b, B5)
  - One - 2" x 5" (A37)
  - Three 2" x 2½" (B2)
  - One - 1¼" x 5" (A30)
  - Two - 1⅝" x 3⅛" (A22)
  - Two - 1¼" x 3⅛" (A5)
  - One - 1¼" x 2¾" (G2)

- One 5¾"-wide strip. From this, cut:
  - One - 5" x 5¾" (A32)
  - One - 5⅛" x 5⅜" (A25)
  - One - 3⅞" x 5⅜" (A19)
  - One - 2½" x 5⅛" (A24)
  - Twelve - 2" x 4¼" (B3)

- One 4⅛"-wide strip. From this, cut:
  - One - 2⅞" x 4½" (A11)
  - Six - 2" x 4¼" (B3)
  - Four - 1¼" x 4¼" (Spacer 40)
  - Three - 2" x 4" (B1)
  - One - 3⅞" x 6⅞" (A20)
  - Three - 2¾" x 3½" (C1, E1b, F1)

Dance Ballerina, Dance

30¾" x 42"
Designed and quilted by Mindy Kettner.
Modeled by Elizabeth Evans.

- One 3³/₄"-wide strip. From this, cut:
    One - 3³/₄" x 23¹/₂" (Spacer 44)
    One - 1⁷/₈" x 3¹/₄" (A28a)
    One - 2¹/₂" x 2⁷/₈" (A10a)
    One - 2" x 2⁷/₈" (A13a)
    One - 2³/₄" square (E1a)
    One - 2¹/₄" x 2³/₄" (D1)
    Two - 2" x 2³/₄" (D4, G4)
    One - 2" x 2⁵/₈" (A27)

- One 2"-wide strip. From this, cut:
    One - 2" x 21¹/₂" (Spacer 42)
    One - 1¹/₄" x 2" (F3)
    One - 1⁷/₈" square (A26a)
    Two - 1⁵/₈" x 1³/₄" (A2)
    Eight - 1⁵/₈" squares (A6a, A10b, A18a, A20b, D5a)

- One 1¹/₄"-wide strip. From this, cut:
    Fifteen - 1¹/₄" squares (A1a, A26b, A28c, C4a, F4a, F5a, G6a, G7, G8a, G9a)
    Eight - ⁷/₈" squares (A4a, A8a, A36a)

From Fabric II, cut: *(dark pink print)*

- One 3⁷/₈"-wide strip. From this, cut:
    One - 3¹/₈" x 4¹/₄" (A21)
    Two - 1⁵/₈" x 2³/₈" (A17)
    One - 1¹/₂" x 5³/₈" (for toe shoe applique #1)
    Two - 1¹/₂" x 26¹/₄" (Border 1)

- Two 1¹/₂"-wide strips. From these, cut:
    Two - 1¹/₂" x 39¹/₂" (Border 2)

From Fabric III, cut: *(dark pink solid)*

- One 2¹/₄"-wide strip. From this, cut:
    One - 2¹/₄" x 7¹/₈" (for toe shoe applique #3)
    One - 1¹/₄" x 2³/₄" (A7)
    Four - ⁷/₈" squares (A35a)
    Two - 1⁵/₈" x 2" (A36)

From Fabric IV, cut: *(light pink print)*

- One 7¹/₄"-wide strip. From this, cut:
    Two - 7¹/₄" squares (pocket and pocket lining)
    Three - 1³/₄" squares (B1b)
    Thirty-six - 2" squares (B1A, B2a, B3a)

- One 2"-wide strip. From this, cut:
    Eight - 2" squares (B3a, B4a, B5a)

From Fabric V, cut: *(white-on-white print)*

- Four 2¹/₂"-wide strips for straight-grain binding.

- One 2⁵/₈"-wide strip. From this, cut:
    One - 2⁵/₈" x 11⁷/₈" (A26)
    One - 1⁷/₈" x 2⁵/₈" (A28b)
    One - 2¹/₂" x 6¹/₂" (A23)
    Two - 2¹/₂" squares (A24b, A25a)
    One - 2" x 6¹/₂" (A18)

- Four 2"-wide strips. From these, cut:
    Two - 2" x 42¹/₂" (Border 4)
    Two - 2" x 28¹/₄" (Border 3)

From Fabric VI, cut: *(light blue print)*

- One 2³/₄"-wide strip. From this, cut:
    One - 2³/₄" x 4¹/₄" (E1)
    Nine - 1¹/₄" x 2³/₄" (C2, D3, F2, G1, G3, G5, G6)
    One - 1" x 2³/₄" (D2)
    Two - 1⁵/₈" squares (D1a)
    Three - 1¹/₄" x 2" (F4, G8)
    Ten - 1¹/₄" squares (C1a, F1a, G2a, G4a)

- One 1¹/₄"-wide strip. From this, cut:
    Eight - 1¹/₄" x 5" (C3, C4, D5, E2, F5, G9)

From Fabric VII, cut: *(solid flesh)*

- One 4¹/₄"-wide strip. From this, cut:
    One - 4¹/₈" x 4¹/₄" (A1)
    One - 2³/₈" x 4¹/₄" (A16)
    One - 3⁷/₈" square (A20a)
    One - 2¹/₂" x 3⁷/₈" (A10)
    One - 2" x 3³/₈" (A13)
    One - 2³/₄" square (A19a)
    Two - 2³/₄" x 5" (A31)
    One - 2¹/₂" square (A24a)
    One - 1⁷/₈" x 5¹/₈" (A28)
    One - 1⁷/₈" x 4¹/₂" (A12)
    One - 1³/₄" x 2" (A3)

- One 2"-wide strip. From this, cut:
    Two - 2" x 8¹/₄" (A35)
    One - 1³/₈" square (A24c)
    Four - ⁷/₈" squares (A34a, A38a, A39a)

From Fabric VIII, cut: *(solid black)*

- One 1⁵/₈"-wide strip. From this, cut:
    One - 1⁵/₈" x 5³/₄" (A6)
    One - 1¹/₂" x 5" (toe shoe applique #2)
    Three - 1¹/₄" x 2³/₄" (A4, A8)
    Two - 1¹/₄" squares (A1b)

Assembly

Block A

1. Use diagonal corner technique (page 8) to make one each of units 1, 4, 6, 8, 18, 19, 20, 24, 25, 26, 34, 35, 36, 38, and 39. Use diagonal corner technique to make one of mirror-image unit 4 as shown. To piece unit 24, join 24a first. Trim seam and press out, then add diagonal corners 24b and 24c.

2. Units 10, 13, and 28 are to be made using both diagonal end (page 10) and diagonal corner technique. To make units 10 and 13, make diagonal ends first, then add diagonal corners. For unit 28, join diagonal ends 28a and 28b, then join diagonal corner 28c.

3. To assemble Block A, begin by joining units 2, 3, and 2 in a row as shown, then join these combined units to bottom of unit 1. Join mirror image units 4 and 5. Add to opposite sides of combined units 1-3. Join unit 6 to top of combined units. Join units 7 and 8, then add unit 9 to opposite sides of combined units 7-8. Join this section to top of hair, forming the bun to complete the head section.

4. Join units 11 and 12 together as illustrated, then add unit 13 to top of these combined units and unit 10 to the bottom. Join unit 14 to the right side. Join this arm section to right side of head section, and unit 15 to left side to complete top section.

5. For tutu section, begin by joining units 17, 16, and 17 as shown, then add unit 18 to bottom of these combined units.

6. Cut a piece of netting for sleeves 6½" x 20". Fold in half lengthwise. Gather long edge to 3¾". Cut it half and sew into each arm seam. Place one section of gathered netting, right sides together with raw edges matching, between combined units 16-18 and unit 19. Join unit 19 to right side of bodice, stitching netting into seam. Repeat this procedure for unit 20, joining it to left side of bodice. Join bodice top section to bottom of head section, pinning netting out of the way so it is not sewn into the seam.

7. Cut an 11" x 46" piece of netting. Fold in half lengthwise and gather long edge ot 6 ¼". Join units 22, 21, and 22. Place tutu netting, right sides together with raw edges matching, between combined units 21-22 and unit 23. Join unit 23, stitching netting into seam. Join unit 24 to left side of combined units, pinning netting out of the way. Join unit 25 to right side of combined units, again pinning netting out of the way. Join units 26 and 27, then join

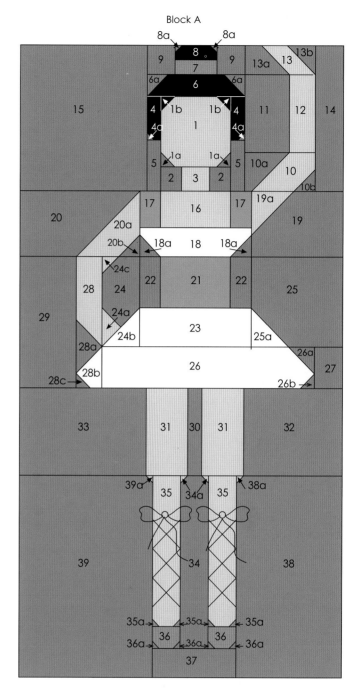

Block A

to bottom of combined units 21-25, pinning netting so that it does not catch in seams. Join units 28 and 29, then add to left side of combined tutu units.

8. For leg section, begin by joining units 33, 31, 30, 31, and 32 in a row as shown. Join to bottom of tutu section, pinning netting out of the way. Join units 35 and 36 as illustrated, then join combined leg and shoe units with unit 34 in the center. Join unit 37 to bottom of leg units. Join unit 38 to right side and unit 39 to left side. Join this leg bottom section to leg top section matching seams to complete block A.

9. Trace face (page 22) using fine tipped fabric pens for the face and white paint for white areas in the eyes.

10. For arm and skirt netting, we used fabric glue to glue ends under to keep netting in place.

DANCE Blocks
Block C:

1. Begin by using diagonal corner technique to make one of units 1 and 4. Join units 2 to top and bottom of unit 1 as shown; then add unit 3 to left side and unit 4 to right side to complete letter "D."

Block D:

2. Use diagonal corner technique to make one of unit 1. Join units 2, 1, 3, and 4 in a vertical row as shown. Join units 5 to opposite sides of combined units; then add diagonal corners 5a to complete letter "A."

Block E:

3. Use diagonal end technique to make one of unit 1, then add units 2 to opposite sides of unit 1 as shown to complete letter "N."

Block F:

4. Use diagonal corner technique to make one each of units 1 and 5. Use diagonal corner technique to make two of mirror image unit 4. Join units 2, 1, and 2 in a row as shown. Join units 4, 3 and 4 in a row; then join to right side of combined units 1-2. Join unit 5 to left side to complete letter "C."

Block G:

5. Use diagonal corner technique to make one each of units 2, 4, 6, 8, and 9. Join units 1, 2, 3, 4, and 5 in a vertical row as shown. Join units 6, 7, and 8 in a vertical row. Join combined units 6-8 to right side of combined units 1-5, then add unit 9 to left side of combined units to complete letter "E."

6. Refer to quilt illustration and join one unit 40 between each letter in the word DANCE. Add unit 41 to the bottom. Join DANCE to left side of ballerina, then join unit 42 across top.

B Block Border

1. For short border on left side of quilt, begin by placing units B5 and B5a right sides together. Stitch a diagonal line from corner to corner. Trim seam and press open. Use diagonal corner technique to make two of unit 3 and one of unit 2. Join units together in a vertical row as shown, then add unit 43 to right side of combined units. Join unit 44 to bottom of combined units; then add to left side of quilt as shown.

2. For right side B border, use diagonal corner technique to make eight of unit 3 and two of mirror-image unit 2. Refer

to quilt illustration and join these blocks together in a vertical row as shown. Join to right side of quilt.

3. For top B border, use diagonal corner technique to make five of unit 3 and two of mirror-image unit 1. Join the units together in a horizontal row as shown in quilt illustration. Join to top of quilt.

4. For B border bottom, use diagonal corner technique to make three of unit 3, and one each of units 1 and 4. Join units in a horizontal row as shown and join to bottom of quilt.

5. Refer to ballet shoe appliqué pattern on page 22. Trace each piece onto paper side of appliqué film. Be sure to include dashed line areas for pieces #1 and #2. Place appliqué pieces on pocket in numerical order. Fuse in place and satin stitch around raw edges of ballet shoe,

6. Place pocket and pocket lining right sides together. Stitch around three sides. Turn pocket right side out and top stitch along the stitched edges.

7. Center pocket under word DANCE as shown, with raw pocket edges matching raw edge of bottom border. Top stitch pocket to quilt along sides only, securing at pocket top.

Finishing

1. Join border 1 to top and bottom of quilt, catching pocket bottom into seam. Join border 2 to opposite sides of quilt. Join Border 3 to top and bottom of quilt; then add border 4 to opposite sides.

2. Ballerina legs are embellished with ribbon X's. Use fabric glue to glue ribbon to legs as shown in drawing. Tie two bows and glue to top of laced "X" ribbon.

3. Quilt as desired. We stitched in-the-ditch by machine, making the quilting an easy task.

4. Bind with 150" of french fold binding from Fabric V.

5. Have fun with the trim and embellish the dancer as desired. We selected a lovely, pointed 1⅜"-wide trim and were able to cut it into a crown for the ballerina's bun and into trim for across bottom of the skirt. Use fabric glue. The heart lace trim was cut apart and used across the top of the bodice, on the shoes, and for earrings. We cut pearls for additional embellishment.

6. We tied a bow for the top of the appliquéd toe shoe, leaving streamers that we twisted and glued down inside pocket on the quilt bottom. We glued a lace heart on the shoe front and placed ribbon roses in the hair, at the neck (with ribbon and a lace heart), and on the shoes.

Quilt Top Assembly

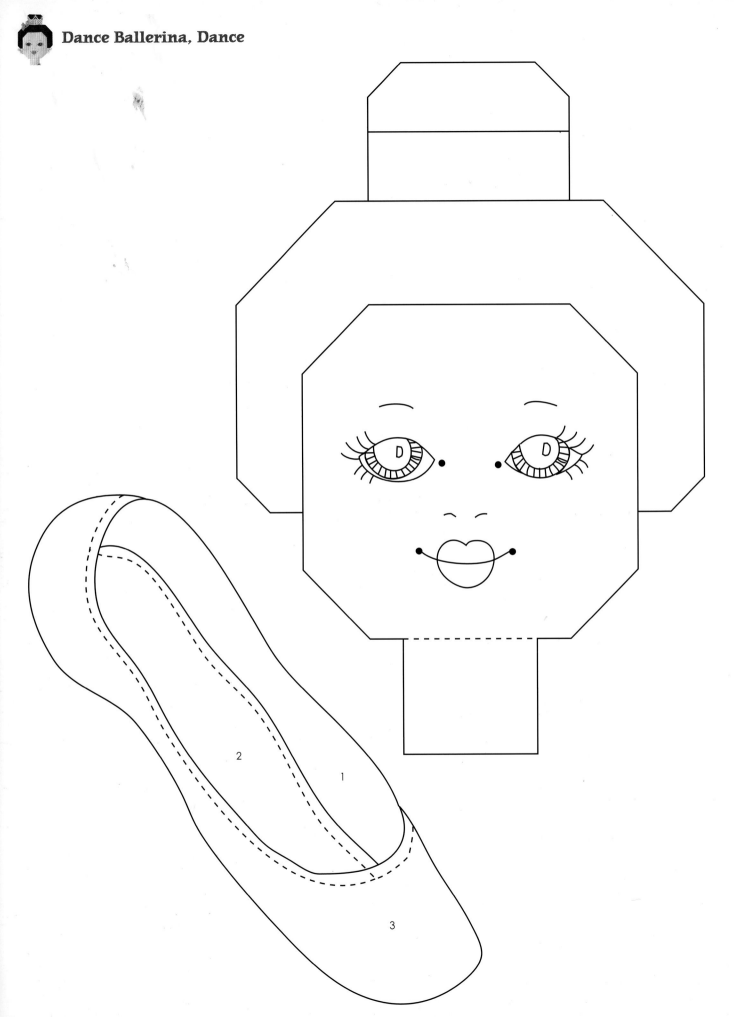

Dance Ballerina, Dance

Dreams of Gold

FABRIC TIPS In selecting fabrics for our gymnasts, we chose a nice light-medium solid blue for one background and a light yellow texture print for the other. This helps the gymnasts "pop" out of the backgrounds and get your immediate attention. For such an important performance, we chose bright, happy colors for their leotards. Gold and dark brown texture prints were just right for hair. Our border is a soft green that contrasts nicely with the other background colors. Border hearts in bright colors lead your eye to the names of your gymnasts (optional), while red and white hearts at the center add interest to otherwise blank areas.

Materials

Fabric I	(light blue solid)	$1^7/8$ yards
Fabric II	(light yellow texture print)	$1^7/8$ yards
Fabric III	(medium yellow print)	$3/4$ yard
Fabric IV	(solid medium-dark green)	$3/4$ yard
Fabric V	(grain rust print)	$1/4$ yard
Fabric VI	(solid black)	$1/4$ yard
Fabric VII	(medium green print)	$3^1/2$ yards
Fabric VIII	(bright red print)	$3/8$ yard
Fabric IX	(white-on-white print)	$1/4$ yard
Fabric X	(solid bright pink)	$1/2$ yard
Fabric XI	(medium blue print)	$1/4$ yard
Dark gold print and light gold print		scraps
Scraps of mixed skin tones for body parts		$1/2$ yard
Appliqué film		4 yards
Tear-away stabilizer		4 yards
Backing		$6^1/8$ yards
Batting		78" x 109"

- Fabric pens to draw eyes, mouth, and eyelashes
- Glittery fabric paint to put names of gymnasts in border hearts (optional)
- Satin ribbons for hair bows

Dreams Of Gold

64"x 99" without scallops
72" x 103" with scallops
Designed by Robert and Pam Bono
(from a concept by Mindy Kettner).
Quilted by Faye Gooden.

Cutting

From Fabric I, cut: (light blue solid)

- One $16^3/4$" -wide strip. From this, cut:
  Two - $16^3/4$" x $20^1/2$" (A6)

- One $10^1/4$" -wide strip. From this, cut:
  Two - $10^1/4$" x $17^3/4$" (E3)
  Two - $3^1/2$" x $6^3/4$" (C5)
  Two - $1^1/2$" x 2" (C3)

- Two $9^1/2$"-wide strips. From these, cut:
  One - $9^1/2$" x $18^1/2$" (C1)
  One - $9^1/2$" x 18" (E1)

**Cut one $9^1/2$" piece above from each strip so you will have enough fabric for $9^1/4$" cuts.
  Two - $9^1/4$" x 22" (C2)

- One $6^3/4$"-wide strip. From this, cut:
  Two - $6^3/4$" x 16" (C7)
  Two - 2" x $6^3/4$" (C8)

- One $4^1/2$" -wide strip. From this, cut:
  One - $4^1/2$" x $10^1/2$" (A1)
  Two - $4^1/2$" x $12^1/2$" (A3)
- Two $2^1/2$" wide strips. From these, cut:
  Two - $2^1/2$" x 22" (C9)
  One - $1^1/2$" x $12^1/2$" (A5)

From Fabric II, cut: (light yellow texture print)

- One $18^1/4$"-wide strip. From this, cut:
  One - $18^1/4$" x $35^1/2$" (D1)
  Two - 3" x 4" (B12)
  Two - $2^1/2$" x 5" (B18)
  Two - $1^1/4$" x 5" (B16)
  Two - $1^1/2$" x $4^3/4$" (D5)
  Two - $1^1/2$" x 3" (B10)
  Two - $1^1/2$" x $2^1/2$" (D7)

- One 10½"-wide strip. From this, cut:
  One - 10½" x 13" (B30)
  One - 3½" x 21" (B25)
  One - 2½" x 21" (B8)
  Two - 3¼" x 5½" (D10)
  One - 3" x 9" (B14)

- One 9¼"-wide strip. From this, cut:
  One - 9¼" x 17½" (B9)
  One - 4½" x 9¼" (B28)
  One - 2½" x 9¼" (B29)
  Two - 2¼" x 9" (D11)
  One - 5" x 9" (B20)
  One - 1½" x 8½" (B7)
  One - 3½" x 5½" (B5)
  Two - 1¼" x 3½" (B3)
  Two - 2" x 2¼" (B23)
  Two - 1¼" x 1½" (B21)

- One 9"-wide strip. From this, cut:
  Two - 9" x 12¼" (D4)
  One - 3¼" x 14½" (B24)
  One - 2¼" x 14½" (B32)

- One 8½"-wide strip. From this, cut:
  One - 8½" x 14¼" (B1)
  One - 8¼" x 16½" (B26)
  Two - 5½" squares (D8)

- One 5½"-wide strip. From this, cut:
  One - 5½" x 12¼" (B33)
  One - 3½" x 12¼" (B34)

- One 1¼"-wide strip. From this, cut:
  One - 1¼" x 35½" (D3)

From Fabric III, cut: (medium yellow print)

- One 23" x 42" piece for border hearts, Olympic hearts, and leotards

From Fabric IV, cut: (solid medium-dark green)

- One 7½"-wide strip. From this, cut:
  One - 7½" x 14½" (Olympic hearts)

- Cut remainder into three 2½"-wide strips.
  From these, cut:
  Three - 2½" x 26½" (center sashing) piece together pairs to equal 52½" strips.

- Five 2½"-wide strips. From these, cut:
  Five - 2½" x 26½" (center sashing) piece as above.

- One - 1¼"-wide strip. From this, cut:
  One - 1¼" x 18" (E2)

From Fabric V, cut: (grain rust print)

- One 2"-wide strip. From this, cut:
  One - 2" x 8½" (B2)
  One - 1½" x 17½" (B15)

- Three 1½"-wide strips. From these, cut:
  One - 1½" x 35½" (D2)
  Two - 1½" x 2¾" (D6)
  Two - 1½" x 20½" (C4)
  One - 1½" x 12½" (B11)
  One - 1½" x 16½" (B27)

From Fabric VI, cut: (solid black)

- Three 1¼"-wide strips. From these, cut:
  Two - 1¼" x 10½" (B31)
  Four - 1¼" x 6¾" (C6)
  Two - 1¼" x 5½" (D9)
  Four - 1¼" x 5" (B17, B19)
  Two - 1¼" x 3½" (B4)
  Two - 1¼" x 3" (B13)
  Two - 1¼" x 1½" (B22)

- One 1"-wide strip. From this, cut:
  Twelve - 1" x 3½" (beam bases) Follow instructions on pattern for cutting corners.
  Use extra fabric for hair and leotards.

From Fabric VII, cut: (medium green print)

- One 6⅞"-wide strip. From this, cut:
  One - 6⅞" square (border 5) cut in half diagonally into two triangles.

  Cut remainder into four 1½" strips. From these, cut:
  Two - 1½" x 32½" (border 7)
  Two - 1½" x 26½" (border 8)
- One 6⅜" wide strip. From this, cut:
  Five - 6⅜" squares (border 4) Cut in half diagonally into ten triangles.

- Seven 5½"-wide strips. From these, cut:
  Ten - 5½" x 8½" (border 3)
  Twenty-six - 5½" x 6½" (border 1)

- Two 5"-wide strips. From these, cut:
  Thirteen - 5" squares (border 2) Cut in half diagonally into twenty-six triangles.
- Five 1½"-wide strips for borders 6.
- 1½ yards for bias binding

From Fabric VIII, cut: (bright red print)

  One - 1½" x 8½" (B6)
  One 10½" x 24" piece for center hearts, Olympic hearts, and leotards

From Fabric IX, cut: (white-on-white print)

• One - 9" x 18" piece for center hearts and leotards

From Fabric X, cut: (solid bright pink)

• One 16"-wide strip for border hearts, Olympic hearts and leotards

From Fabric XI, cut: (medium blue print)

• One 7 1/2" x 14 1/2" for Olympic hearts and leotards

Cut from the following fabrics:

• From scrap, cut: (dark gold)
    One - 4 1/2" x 5 3/4" (A2)

• From scrap, cut: (light gold)
    Two - 3 3/4" x 4 1/2" (A4)

Please follow instructions on patterns for cutting body parts from the fabrics of your choice.

Assembly

Section A

1. Refer to illustration for section A and begin by joining units 1 and 2. Join units 3 and 4. Join the 3-4 units to opposite sides of center unit 1-2; then add unit 5 to bottom. Join unit 6 to opposite sides of center unit to complete section A.

Section B

1. Refer to illustration for section B and begin by joining units 1 and 2. Join units 3, 4, 5, 4, and 3 in a row as shown, then add combined units 1-2 to top of this row. Join units 6 and 7 and add to bottom of combined units to complete center section.

2. For left side of section B, join units 10, 11, and 10 in a horizontal row; then add unit 9 to top of this row. Join units 12, 13, 14, 13, and 12 in another horizontal row. Join to combined units 9-11, then add unit 15 to bottom of this section. Join units 16, 17, 18, 19, 20, 19, 18, 17, and 16 in a horizontal row as shown. Join this row to combined units 9-15, matching the legs of the parallel bars.

3. Join units 21 and 22 as shown, then add unit 23 to bottom. Join these combined units to opposite sides of unit 24, keeping in mind that the 21-22 units are mirror images. Join the resulting section to bottom of parallel bars, matching legs.

4. Join unit 8 to left side of parallel bars and unit 25 to right side.

5. To assemble high bar section, begin by joining units 26 and 27, then add unit 28 to left side of combined units and unit 29 to right side. Join units 31, 30, and 31 in a horizontal row as shown, then add unit 32 to bottom of combined units. Join unit 33 to left side of combined units 30-32 and join unit 34 to right side. Join top of resulting section to bottom of high bar section.

6. Join parallel bar section to left side of center section and high bar section to right side to complete section B. Refer to page 11 for instructions on use of appliqué film and center beam bases at bottom of each beam. Press in place and satin stitch around beam bases (see photo page 23). Place tear-away stabilizer behind all appliqués.

Section C

1. For assembly of balance beams, begin by joining units 3 and 4 as shown. Join unit 2 to top of combined units 3-4. Be sure to place 3-4 units as shown in diagram as they are mirror images.

2. Join units 5, 6, 7, 6, and 8 in a row as shown. Make two, reversing order for second mirror-image set. Join unit 9 to bottom of these combined units. Join the top section of balance beams to the bottom section, then join each balance beam section to opposite sides of unit 1.

3. Refer to step 6 above, and satin stitch beam bases.

Section D

1. Refer to illustration for section D and join units 1, 2, and 3 together as shown. For side balance beams, begin by joining units 5, 6, and 7 in a row. Make two, reversing order for second mirror image set.

2. Join units 8, 9, and 10 in a row. Make two, reversing order for second mirror image set as shown. Join these combined units to combined units 5-7, referring frequently to illustration for correct placement of mirror image. Join unit 4 to top of combined units and unit 11 to bottom.

3. Join balance beam sections to opposite sides of center floor exercise section, unit 1.

4. Refer to section B, step 6 above and satin stitch beam bases in place.

Section E

1. Join units 1 and 2, then add unit 3 to opposite sides of combined 1-2 units to complete section E.

Section A

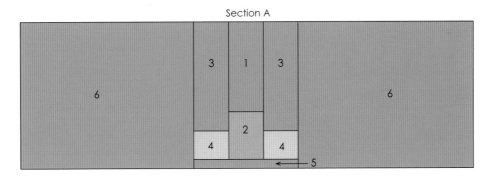

Section B

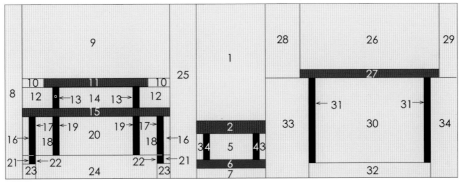

Section C

Section D

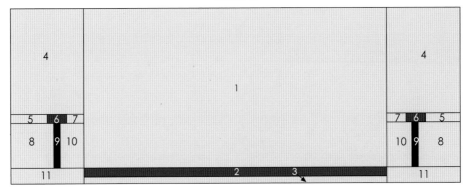

Section E

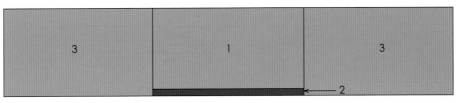

Placement of Gymnasts and Hearts

1. All gymnasts will be fused to the background with appliqué film. See page 11 for instructions.

2. Refer to the photographs for suggested placement and color of gymnasts. The gymnast patterns are designed to allow you to dress them according to your preferences and fabric choices.

3. Refer to gymnast pattern pieces on pages 31–33. Cut each piece on solid lines. Dashed lines show where the particular pattern piece fits under another piece. The small drawings of each gymnast are numbered to show the order in which appliqué pieces should be placed, allowing the dashed areas to fit under other pieces to avoid frayed edges.

Dreams of Gold

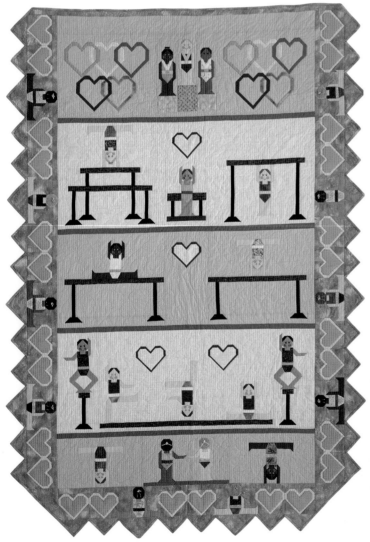

4. Gymnasts on quilt assembly diagram are numbered to be consistant with the small placement drawings of each gymnast. This not only identifies gymnasts on the quilt drawing, but also identifies the correct gymnasts in the small placement drawings.

5. Beginning with section A, please note that all three gymnasts are different, each is an individual with a different colored medal around her neck. They are all cut from the same pattern pieces you used for gymnast #1. Place each gymnast on a stand, laying appliqué pieces down in order given. Move the pieces until you are satisfied with their placement, then press in place.

6. For the Olympic hearts, the quilt assembly diagram (page 30) is marked to show you how to properly center the hearts in the block. Cut hearts from colors of your choice and place them as shown. We suggest using a water-soluble pen to draw lines $1^3/4''$ from the top and bottom of the block and $1^1/2''$ and $1^1/4''$ from sides of block to aid in correct placement of hearts. When you are satisfied with the placement, and all measurements match, press hearts in place. See quilt illustration on page 30.

7. Press cheeks in place on all gymnasts and use embroidery thread or fabric pens to draw eyes, mouth, and eyelashes. Place tear-away stabilizer behind all appliqués and pin in place. Satin stitch around all appliqués.

8. Place and press all gymnasts in section B. Draw a line $2^1/4''$ down from top center of block. Place red heart first, centering it so its point matches center hair line of gymnast #3. Press in place. Center white heart inside red heart and press in place. Use embroidery, satin stitching, or fabric paint for eyes, eyelashes, and mouth to complete gymnasts' faces and satin stitch around all appliqués.

9. Work section C in the same manner as Section B, referring to quilt assembly diagram (page 30) for placement of heart and gymnasts.

10. For section D, please note that gymnasts #6 are mirror images. Placement of hearts is shown on quilt assembly diagram. Use water-soluble pen to draw a line $3^1/4''$ down from top of block in the floor exercise section. Measure 7" in from seams as shown and draw a line to help you place hearts. Press hearts in place and satin stitch around them.

11. Complete section E as you did for other blocks.

12. Make four sets of 2^1/$_2$'' x 52^1/$_2$'' strips from Fabric IV by joining pairs of the 2^1/$_2$'' x 26^1/$_2$'' strips that have been cut. Join the sections of gymnasts by stitching strips between sections as shown.

Heart/Gymnast Border

1. Cut hearts as directed on pattern pieces and use our appliqué film procedure as described on page 11, centering hearts in unit 1 and pressing them in place. Satin stitch all hearts.

2. With right sides together, join triangle 2 to bottom of each heart unit, then join heart units in pairs as shown. Join triangle 4 to bottom of each unit 3 as shown.

3. For bottom border, join three heart pairs, alternating with unit 3 as illustrated.

4. Join the two 1^1/$_2$'' x 26^1/$_2$'' strips of fabric VII, end to end to equal 52^1/$_2$'' long. Join this strip (unit 8) to top of bottom heart section as shown. Press gymnasts #9 in place as illustrated in quilt assembly diagram and satin stitch. Join this completed border to bottom of quilt.

5. For side borders, join five heart pairs alternating with unit 3. For unit 6 strip, join the five 1^1/$_2$'' wide strips of fabric VII end to end. Cut two 94" strips. These strips are a bit longer than needed. Join strip 6 to top edge of side heart border and trim off excess. Place gymnasts as for bottom border and satin stitch in place. Add triangle 5 to bottom edge, checking quilt assembly diagram for correct placement. Make two of these borders and join to sides of quilt, matching corner #5 triangles to bottom border as shown. Trim triangle to straighten if necessary.

6. Join the 1^1/$_2$'' x 32^1/$_2$'' strips of fabric VII, end to end to equal a strip that is 1^1/$_2$'' x 64^1/$_2$''. Join to quilt top and trim corners diagonally as shown to complete quilt top.

7. If you wish to use fabric paint at this time to write names of gymnastic team members in border hearts, follow manufacturer's instructions and allow 24 hours for drying.

Finishing

1. Quilt as desired. Cut 2^1/$_4$''-wide strips of bias binding from 1^1/$_2$ yard piece of fabric VII and join together to create 480" of bias binding.

2. Bind quilt.

3. Make ten small bows from different colors of ^{1}/$_8$'' wide satin ribbon and tack securely to back of all gymnast #9 heads.

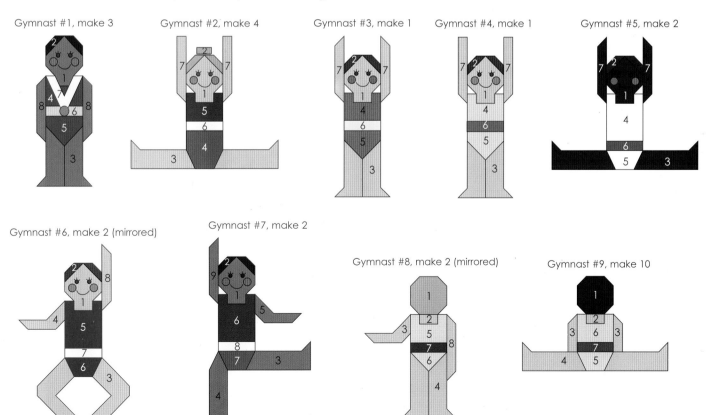

Gymnast #1, make 3

Gymnast #2, make 4

Gymnast #3, make 1

Gymnast #4, make 1

Gymnast #5, make 2

Gymnast #6, make 2 (mirrored)

Gymnast #7, make 2

Gymnast #8, make 2 (mirrored)

Gymnast #9, make 10

 Dreams of Gold

30

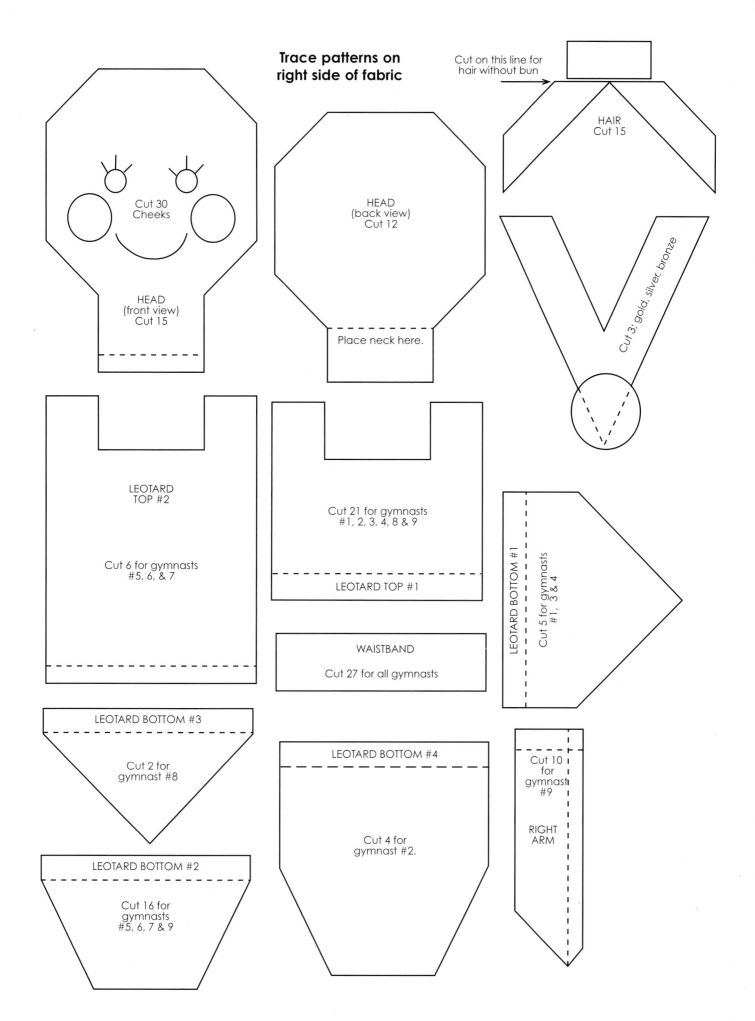

Trace patterns on right side of fabric

Cut 30 Cheeks

HEAD (front view) Cut 15

HEAD (back view) Cut 12

Place neck here.

Cut on this line for hair without bun

HAIR Cut 15

Cut 3: gold, silver, bronze

LEOTARD TOP #2

Cut 6 for gymnasts #5, 6, & 7

Cut 21 for gymnasts #1, 2, 3, 4, 8 & 9

LEOTARD TOP #1

LEOTARD BOTTOM #1

Cut 5 for gymnasts #1, 3 & 4

WAISTBAND

Cut 27 for all gymnasts

LEOTARD BOTTOM #3

Cut 2 for gymnast #8

LEOTARD BOTTOM #4

Cut 4 for gymnast #2.

Cut 10 for gymnast #9

RIGHT ARM

LEOTARD BOTTOM #2

Cut 16 for gymnasts #5, 6, 7 & 9

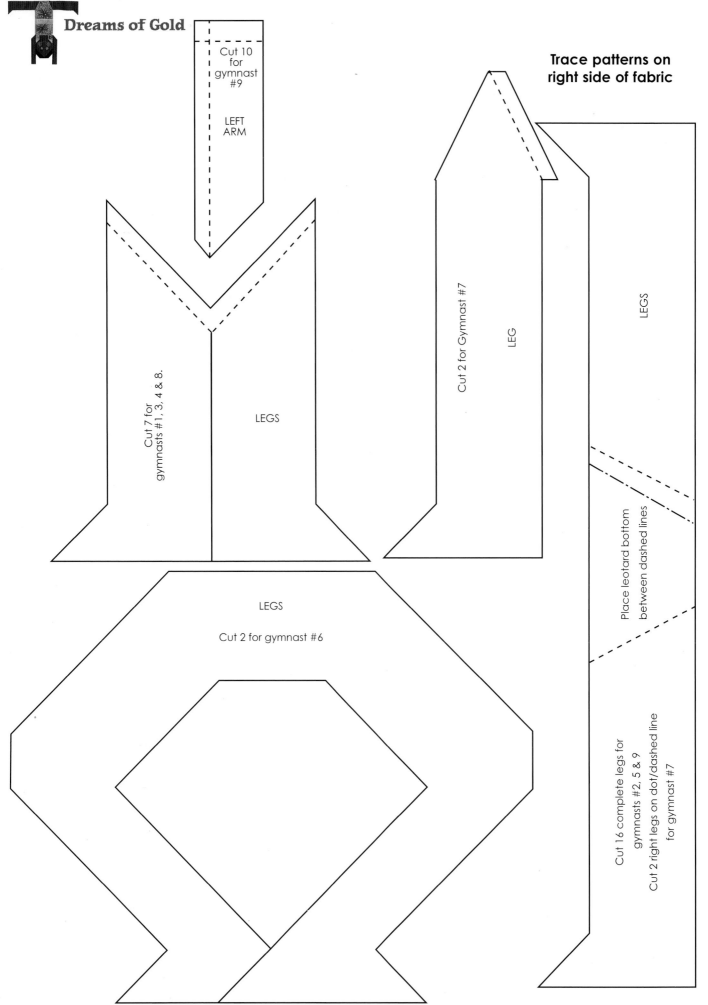

Dreams of Gold

Cut 10 for gymnast #9

LEFT ARM

Trace patterns on right side of fabric

Cut 7 for gymnasts #1, 3, 4 & 8.

LEGS

Cut 2 for Gymnast #7

LEG

LEGS

Place leotard bottom between dashed lines

LEGS

Cut 2 for gymnast #6

Cut 16 complete legs for gymnasts #2, 5 & 9

Cut 2 right legs on dot/dashed line for gymnast #7

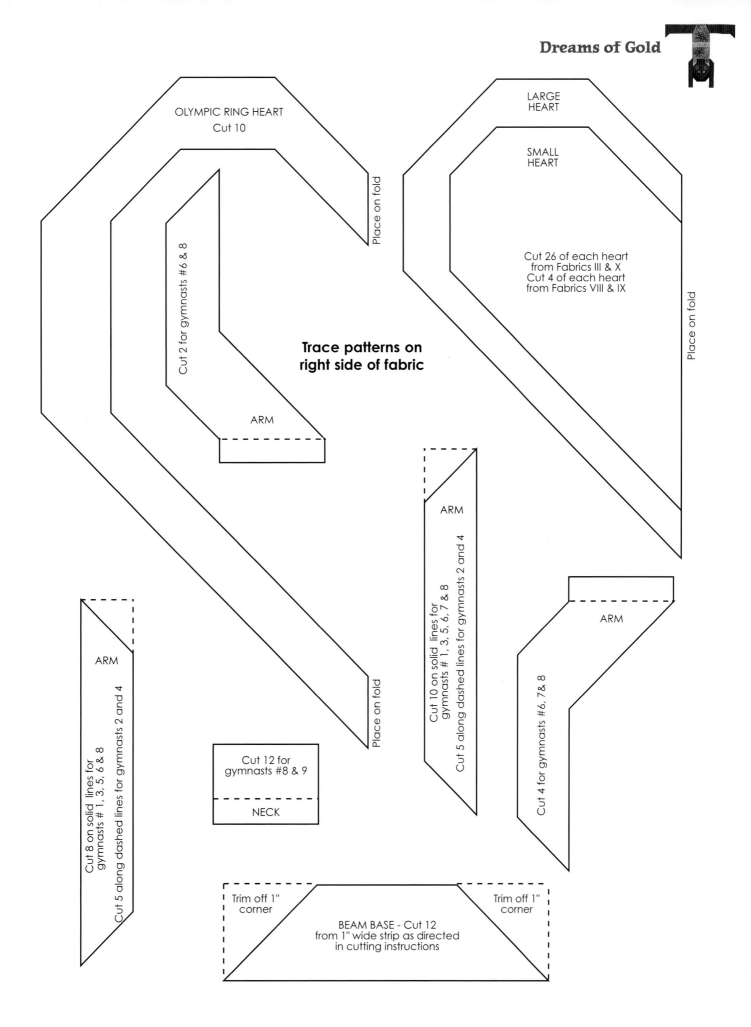

OLYMPIC RING HEART
Cut 10

LARGE
HEART

SMALL
HEART

Cut 26 of each heart
from Fabrics III & X
Cut 4 of each heart
from Fabrics VIII & IX

Place on fold

Place on fold

Cut 2 for gymnasts #6 & 8

**Trace patterns on
right side of fabric**

ARM

ARM

ARM

ARM

Cut 10 on solid lines for
gymnasts # 1, 3, 5, 6, 7 & 8
Cut 5 along dashed lines for gymnasts 2 and 4

Cut 4 for gymnasts #6, 7 & 8

Place on fold

Cut 8 on solid lines for
gymnasts # 1, 3, 5, 6 & 8
Cut 5 along dashed lines for gymnasts 2 and 4

Cut 12 for
gymnasts #8 & 9

NECK

Trim off 1"
corner

Trim off 1"
corner

BEAM BASE - Cut 12
from 1" wide strip as directed
in cutting instructions

Elephants on Parade

Materials

■ Fabric I	(dark gray print)	1½ yards
■ Fabric II	(pale green print)	3 yards
■ Fabric III	(solid medium gray)	½ yard
■ Fabric IV	(light gray print)	⅜ yard
□ Fabric V	(ivory print)	1⅜ yards
■ Fabric VI	(gray on black print)	¼ yard
■ Fabric VII	(dark green print)	1¼ yards
■ Fabric VIII	(medium green print)	⅞ yard
■ Fabric IX	(magenta print)	¼ yard
■ Fabric X	(bright pink print)	¼ yard
■ Fabric XI	(dark blue print)	⅜ yard
■ Fabric XII	(light blue print)	½ yard
□ Fabric XIII	(solid bright yellow)	¼ yard
□ Fabric XIV	(light yellow print)	1⅝ yards
■ Fabric XV	(bright orange print)	⅛ yard
■ Fabric XVI	(peach print)	⅛ yard
Fabric XVII	(12 large scraps or fat quarters of different decorative fabrics for elephant adornments to coordinate with flower colors Fabrics IX-XVI)	
Backing		6 yards
Batting		72" x 108"
Colored trim		scraps
Tassels, ribbon, and studs		miscellaneous
Appliqué film and tear-away pellon		large scraps

Elephants on Parade

66" x 102"
Elephant blocks: 27" square
Flower blocks: 4½" x 9"
Designed by Pam Bono.
Quilted by Faye Gooden.

FABRIC TIPS ▶

Bright colors used in the right places are the key to this design. We found a wonderful gray batik that looks like an elephant's skin texture and makes the elephants come alive. A pale olive print in the elephant background makes the elephants stand out, and the darker olive print borders with their brightly colored flowers emphasize the elephants as the main focal point. We dressed up each elephant with jazzy tassels and trims.

Cutting

■ From Fabric I, cut: (dark gray print)

- One 6¼"-wide strip. From this, cut:
  Six - 5¼" x 6¼" (A50, B50)
  Six - 1½" x 6¼" (A41, B41)

- Two 5½"-wide strips. From these and scrap, cut:
  Six - 5½" x 9¼" (A9, B9)
  Six - 2¾" x 5½" (A4, B4)
  Six - 2" x 5½" (A37, B37)

- Two 3¾"-wide strips. From these, cut:
  Six - 3¾" x 6½" (A8, B8)
  Six - 3¾" squares (A2a, B2a)
  Six - 2" x 3¾" (A3a, B3a)
  Six - 1¼" x 3¾" (A68, B68)

- Three 3½"-wide strips. From this, cut:
  Six - 3½" x 4" (A38, B38)
  Six - 2" x 3¼" (A51, B51)
  Six - 3¼" x 8½" (A26, B26)

- Cut remainder into three 1" wide strips.
  From these, cut:
  Eighteen - 1" squares (A24a, B24a, A53b, B53b, A74a, B74a)

- Two 3"-wide strips. From these, cut:
  Six - 1½" x 3" (A21, B21)
  Six - 1¾" x 2¾" (A76, B76)
  Six - 1¾" x 2½" (A78, B78)

- Two 2¼"-wide strips. From these, cut:
  Six - 2" x 2¼" (A52, B52)
  Six - 1¾" x 2¼" (A73, B73)
  Six - 2¼" squares (A75a, B75a)
  Six - 1½" x 2¾" (A56, B56)
  Twelve - 2" squares (A7a, B7a)
  Six - 1¼" x 2" (A54, B54)

- One 1¾"-wide strip. From this, cut:
  Six - 1¾" x 4¾" (A47, B47)
  Six - 1½" x 2" (A35, B35)

Elephants on Parade

- One 1½"-wide strip. From this, cut:
  Eighteen - 1½" squares (A1a, B1a, A40b, B40b, A51b, B51b)

- One 1¼"-wide strip. From this, cut:
  Thirty - 1¼" squares (A3b, B3b, A20a, B20a, A36a, B36a, A66a, B66a)

- One 1"-wide strip. From this and scraps, cut:
  Twelve - 1" x 2" (A5a, B5a, A23, B23)

From Fabric II, cut: (pale green print)

- Five 5¼"-wide strips. From these, cut:
  Six - 5¼" x 7¾" (A66, B66)
  Six - 5¼" x 7½" (A79, B79)
  Six - 5¼" squares (A49, B49)
  Six - 2¼" x 5" (A53a, B53a)
  Six - 1¾" x 4¾" (A19, B19)
  Six - 2" x 4¼" (A12, B12)

- Four 4¼"-wide strips. From these, cut:
  Six - 4¼" x 10½" (A34, B34)
  Six - 4¼" x 8¾" (A65, B65)
  Six - 2½" x 4¼" (A10, B10)
  Six - 2½" x 4" (A64, B64)
  Six - 2" x 4" (A43, B43)
  Six - 1" x 3" (A16, B16)

- Three 3¾"-wide strips. From these, cut:
  Six - 3¾" x 4½" (A67, B67)
  Six - 3¾" squares (A8a, B8a)
  Six - 3½" x 3¾" (A39, B39)
  Six - 2" x 2¾" (A29, B29)

- One 3½"-wide strip. From this, cut:
  Six - 2¾" x 3½" (A75, B75)
  Six - 2½" x 3½" (A33, B33)

- Six 3¼"-wide strips. Out of each strip, cut:
  One - 3¼" x 26¾" (A80, B80)
  One - 3¼" x 8½" (A27, B27)
  One - 3¼" square (A9a, B9a)
  One - 1½" x 3¼" (A70, B70)
  One - 1¼" x 3¼" (A25, B25)
  When all six strips have been cut, you should have six of each unit.

- One 2½"-wide strip. From this, cut:
  Six - 2½" x 3" (A72, B72)
  Six - 1½" x 2" (A13a, B13a)
  Six - 2" x 2¼" (A62, B62)

- Four 2"-wide strips. From these, cut:
  Six - 2" x 13" (A18, B18)
  Twenty-four - 2" squares (A38a, B38a, A52a, B52a, A55, B55, A57a, B57a)
  Six - 1¾" x 2" (A22, B22)
  Six - 1" x 2¼" (A5c, B5c)
  Six - 1" x 2" (A28, B28)
  Six - 1" x 1¾" (A6a, B6a)

- Three 1¾"-wide strips. From these, cut:
  Six - 1¾" x 6½" (A44, B44)
  Six - 1¾" x 3" (A76a, B76a)
  Six - 1¾" x 2¾" (A77, B77)
  Six - 1¾" squares (A73a, B73a)
  Twelve - 1¼" x 1¾" (A60a, B60a, A71a, B71a)

- Two 1½"-wide strips. From these, cut:
  Six - 1½" x 3" (A14, B14)
  Six - 1½" x 2¾" (A31, B31)
  Eighteen - 1½" squares (A13b, B13b, A32b, B32b, A56a, B56a)

- Six 1¼"-wide strips. From these, cut:
  Six - 1¼" x 27½" (A81, B81)
  Fifty-four - 1¼" squares (A17a, B17a, A26a, B26a, A36b, B36b, A38b, B38b, A42a, B42a, A78a, B78a)

- One 1"-wide strip. From this, cut:
  Forty-two - 1" sq. (A23a, B23a, A24b, B24b, A28b, B28b, A32a, B32a, A60b, B60b, A63a, B63b)

From Fabric III, cut: (solid medium gray)

- One 5½"-wide strip. From this, cut:
  Six - 5½" x 6½" (A1, B1)

- One 4½"-wide strip. From this, cut:
  Six - 2¼" x 4½" (A40, B40)
  Twelve - 2" x 3¾" (A3, B3, A17, B17)

- Two 2"-wide strips. From these, cut:
  Six - 2" x 6¼" (A45, B45)
  Six - 1¼" x 1¾" (A48, B48)
  Twelve - 1¼" squares (A46a, B46a, A50a, B50a)
  Six - 1" x 2" (A5b, B5b)

From Fabric IV, cut: (light gray print)

- One 3"-wide strip. From this, cut:
  Six - 3" x 3½" (A57, B57)
  Six - 2" x 3" (A42, B42)
  Six - 1" x 2½" (A59, B59)

- One 2¼"-wide strip. From this, cut:
  Six - 2¼" x 4" (A40a, B40a)
  Six - 1" x 2¼" (A63, B63)
  Six - 2" squares (A53c, B53c)

- One 2"-wide strip. From this, cut:
  Six - 2" x 4½" (A36, B36)
  Six - 1¾" squares (A74, B74)

- One 1¾"-wide strip. From this, cut:
  Six - 1¾" x 6¼" (A58, B58)

- One 1½"-wide strip. From this, cut:
  Six - 1½" squares (A41a, B41a)
  Eighteen - 1¼" squares (A4a, B4a, A40c, B40c, A44a, B44a)

- One 1"-wide strip. From this, cut:
  Twelve - 1" squares (A61a, B61a, A65a, B65a)

 *From Fabric V, cut: (ivory print)*

- Four 5"-wide strips. From these, cut:
  Eighty-four - 2" x 5" (C5, D5, E5, F5)

- One 2³/₄"-wide strip. From this, cut:
  Six - 2" x 2³/₄" (A51a, B51a)
  Six - 1¹/₄" x 2³/₄" (A71, B71)
  Six - 2¹/₄" x 3" (A53, B53)

- Eight 2"-wide strips. From these, cut:
  168 - 2" squares (C2b, D2b, E2b, F2b, C4, D4, E4, F4)

- One 1¹/₄"-wide strip. From this, cut:
  Six - 1¹/₄" x 3¹/₄" (A69, B69)
  Eighteen - 1¹/₄" squares (A67a, B67a, A68a, B68a, A72a, B72a)

■ *From Fabric VI, cut: (gray on black print)*

- Two 1³/₄"-wide strips. From these, cut:
  Six - 1³/₄" x 4³/₄" (A20, B20)
  Six - 1³/₄" x 3" (A61, B61)
  Six - 1³/₄" x 2¹/₄" (A24, B24)
  Six - 1¹/₂" x 2³/₄" (A32, B32)

- One 1¹/₂"-wide strip. From this, cut:
  Six - 1¹/₂" x 2" (A13, B13)
  Six - 1¹/₄" x 2¹/₂" (A60, B60)
  Six - 1¹/₄" squares (A19a, B19a)
  Six - 1" x 1¹/₂" (A28a, B28a)

- Two 1"-wide strips. From these, cut:
  Six - 1" x 4¹/₄"(A11, B11)
  Six - 1"x 3" (A15, B15)
  Six - 1" x 2³/₄" (A30, B30)
  Twelve - 1" squares (A10a, B10a, A19b, B19b)

■ *From Fabric VII, cut: (dark green print)*

- Four 3¹/₂"-wide strips. From these, cut:
  Eighty-four - 2" x 3¹/₂" (C2, D2, E2, F2)

- Twelve 2"-wide strips. From these, cut:
  252 - 2" squares (C1, D1, E1, F1, C3a, D3a, E3a, F3a, C5a, D5a, E5a, F5a)

■ *From Fabric VIII, cut: (medium green print)*
- Seven 3¹/₂"-wide strips. From these, cut:
  Eighty-four - 3¹/₂" squares (C6, D6, E6, F6)

■ *From Fabric IX, cut: (magenta print)*
- Two 2"-wide strips. From these, cut:
  Thirty-two - 2" squares (C2a, C3b)

■ *From Fabric X, cut: (bright pink print)*
- One 3¹/₂"-wide strip. From this, cut:
  Sixteen - 2" x 3¹/₂" (C3)

■ *From Fabric XI, cut: (dark blue print)*

- Four 2"-wide strips. From these, cut:
  Eighty - 2" squares (D2a, D3b)

■ *From Fabric XII, cut: (light blue print)*

- Two 2³/₄"-wide strips. From these, cut:
  Twenty - 2³/₄" squares (Border and Sashing squares)

- Two 3¹/₂"-wide strips. From these, cut:
  Forty - 2" x 3¹/₂" (D3)

□ *From Fabric XIII, cut: (solid bright yellow)*

- Two 2"-wide strips. From these, cut:
  Forty - 2" squares (E2a, E3b)

□ *From Fabric XIV, cut: (light yellow print)*

- One 2³/₄"-wide strip. From this cut:
  Fifteen 2³/₄" squares (sashing squares)

- Nine 2³/₄"-wide strips for outer borders
  Cut one 2³/₄" sashing square from one border strip (remaining sashing square)

- Nine 2¹/₂"-wide strips for straight-grain binding

- One 3¹/₂"-wide strip. From this, cut:
  Twenty - 2" x 3¹/₂" (E3)

■ *From Fabric XV, cut: (bright orange print)*

- One 2"-wide strip. From this, cut:
  Sixteen - 2" squares (F2a, F3b)

■ *From Fabric XVI, cut: (peach print)*

- One 2"-wide strip. From this, cut:
  Eight - 2" x 3¹/₂" (F3)

From Fabric XVII, cut:

Select from twelve different decorative fabrics for elephant adornments. We used two different shades on each elephant. Fabric colors should coordinate with flower colors.

- From darker shade of fabric, cut (for each elephant):
  One - 1" x 5¹/₄" (A6, B6)
  One - 6" square (A7, B7)
- From lighter shade of fabric, cut (for each elephant):
  One - 2¹/₂" x 6¹/₄" (A46, B46)
  One - 1³/₄" x 2¹/₂" (A47a, B47a)
  One - 1" x 2¹/₄"(A5, B5)
  One - 1¹/₄" x 5¹/₂" (A2, B2)

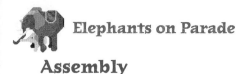

Assembly

Refer closely to the illustration. Reverse for mirror image of the elephant. You will make four elephants facing left (A) and two facing right (B). Should you choose, all elephants may be made facing the same direction. For all elephant sections, instructions given will be for one block only.

Elephant, Section A

1. Use diagonal corner technique on page 8 to make one each of units 1, 4, 7, 8, 9, 10, and 17. Refer to illustration for making combined units 1-2, Section A. To make this unit, join units 1 and 2 as shown. Add diagonal corner 1a, then add diagonal corner 2a as shown in illustration.

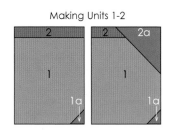

Making Units 1-2

2. Use diagonal end technique (page 10) to make one each of units 3, 5, 6, and 13. Add diagonal corner 3b to unit 3 after completion of diagonal end. Add diagonal corner 13b to unit 13 after completion of diagonal end. Refer to illustration of making unit 5, section A as you make continuous diagonal end unit 5.

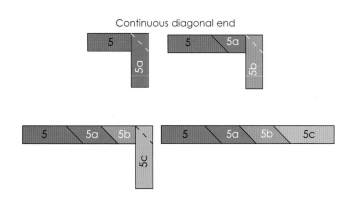

Continuous diagonal end

3. To assemble this section, begin by joining combined units 1-2 with units 3 and 4 in a vertical row; then add unit 5 to top, matching seams. Join units 6 and 7, then add unit 8 to side as shown. Join unit 9 to bottom. Join combined units 1-5 with combined units 6-9.

4. Join units 11 and 12. Join units 14, 15, and 16 as shown. Make a vertical row of units 10, 11-12, 13, and 14-16; then join to elephant.

5. Join units 17 and 18, then join to top of elephant's back to complete section A.

Elephant, Section B

1. Use diagonal corner technique to make one each of units 19, 20, 23, 24, 26, 32, 36, 38, 41, 42, and 44. For unit 36, add diagonal corners in alphabetical order as shown. Use diagonal end technique to make one each of units 28 and 40. To complete unit 28, add diagonal corner 28b after completion of diagonal end. To complete unit 40, once you have completed the diagonal end, join diagonal corners in alphabetical order. Join unit 40b first, press out; then add Unit 40c.

2. To assemble, begin by joining units 19 and 20; then add unit 21 to top of combined units. Join units 22 and 23, then add unit 24 to top, matching seams. Join unit 25 to side of combined units as shown. Join these combined units to combined units 19-21, then add unit 26 as shown.

3. Join units 29 and 30 and units 31 and 32 as shown. Make a vertical row of units 28, 29-30, 31-32, and 33. Join unit 27 to side as shown; then add to combined units 21-26. Join unit 34 to bottom of combined leg/tail units.

4. Join units 35 and 36, then add unit 37. Join units 38 and 39. Join to bottom of combined units 35-37, matching seams. Join combined 35-39 unit to assembled elephant leg.

5. Join units 40 and 41 as shown. Join units 42 and 43, then join unit 44 to side. Join combined units 40-41 with combined units 42-44. Add these combined units to assembled elephant leg to complete Section B.

6. Join sections A and B as shown in photo, matching seams.

Elephant, Section C

1. Use diagonal corner technique to make one of unit 46. Join units 45 and 46. Use diagonal end technique to make one of unit 47 as shown, then add unit 48. Join combined units 47-48 to combined units 45-46 as shown. Add diagonal corner 49 as shown. Trim seam and press outward (head top section).

2. Use diagonal corner technique to make one each of units 50, 52, 56, 57, 61, 63, and 65. Use diagonal end technique to make one each of units 51, 53, and 60. For unit 51, after completion of diagonal end, add diagonal corner 51b. For unit 53 add diagonal corner units 53b and 53c after completion of diagonal end. Add unit 60b to completed unit 60.

3. To assemble this section, begin by joining unit 50 to head top section as shown, matching seam. Join units 51 and 52, then add unit 53 as shown, matching tusk seam.

4. Join units 54 and 55, then add unit 56 to side. Join unit 57 to bottom of these combined units, then join combined

units 51-53 to combined units 54-57, matching seams. Add unit 58 to bottom of combined units. Join the resulting combined unit to head top section.

5. Join units 60 and 61. Join units 62 and 63, then add unit 64 to bottom of units 62-63. Join unit 59 and combined units 60-61 to top of combined units 62-64, then add unit 65 to side. Join this to head top section.

6. Following manufacturer's instructions, trace whites and pupils of elephant eyes onto appliqué film. Press onto appropriate white and black fabric and cut out. Referring to large elephant photo, place eyes as shown on unit 50. Press in place, then pin tear-away pellon behind each eye. Using satin stitch, first stitch the white part of eye, then the black. Stitch white highlight in each eye.

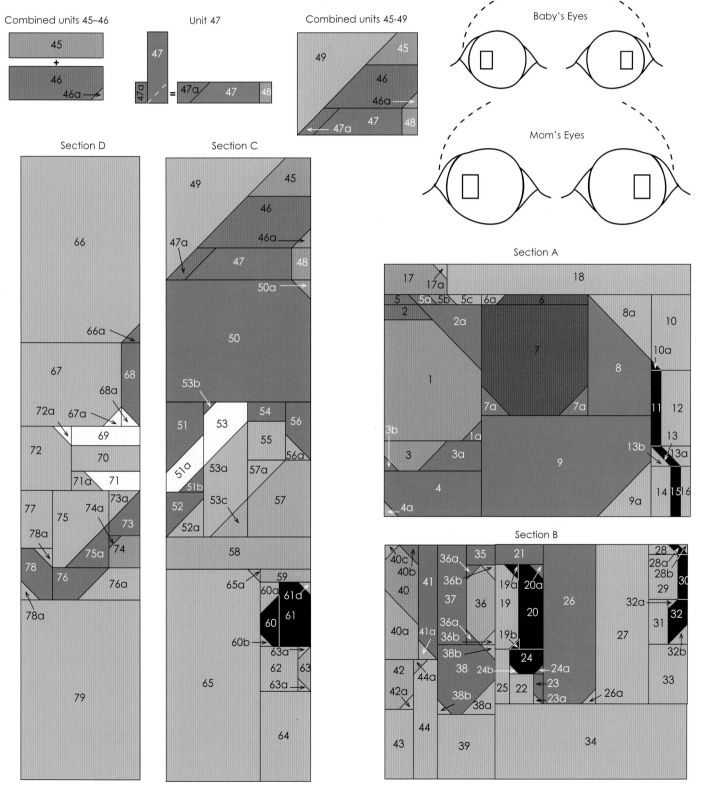

Elephant, Section D

1. Use diagonal corner technique to make one each of units 66, 67, 68, 72, 73, 74, 75, and 78. Use diagonal end technique to make one each of units 71 and 76.

2. To assemble this section, begin by joining units 67 and 68; then add unit 66 to top of these combined units, matching seams. Join units 69, 70, and 71 in a row as shown, then add unit 72 to side, matching seams. Join these combined units to combined units 66-68.

3. Join units 73 and 74, then add unit 75 to side, matching seams. Join unit 76 to bottom of these combined units, matching trunk seam. Join unit 77 and 78, then add to side of combined units 73-76, matching trunk seams. Add unit 79 to bottom as shown, then join all combined units to complete section D. Join sections C and D.

Elephant Assembly

1. Join combined sections A-B with combined sections C-D as shown in photograph. Join background unit 80 to top of elephant as shown in the photograph.

2. Join two elephant blocks together as shown in photo, with tail and trunk seams matching. Press. Add background unit 81 to front of one elephant and back of other.

3. Complete three rows of elephants in this manner.

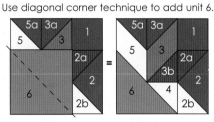

Block C   Use diagonal corner technique to add unit 6.

Flower Blocks

Please refer to illustrations of flower blocks. Each block has two sections as shown for block C. Make each section as follows:

1. Begin with block C. Instructions for assembling block C are the same for all flower blocks. The instructions are for both sides of one flower block (mirror images).

2. Use diagonal corner technique on page 8 to make two each of mirror image units 2, 3, and 5.

3. To assemble, begin by joining units 1 and 2. Join units 3 and 4. Refer to illustration for correct mirror image placement. Join these two rows as shown, then add unit 5. You should now have two mirror-image sides of flower block C.

To complete block, use diagonal corner technique to add unit 6. Trim seam and press. Join the two mirror image sections as shown, matching seams. Make eight of block C, twenty of block D, ten of block E, and four of block F.

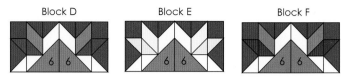

Block D   Block E   Block F

4. Refer to illustration of sashing squares and join 2¾" squares of fabrics XII and XIV as shown. Make eight sashing square blocks and set aside.

Sashing Squares

2 ¾" sq.

Quilt Top Assembly

1. Refer to the photograph. Join flower blocks in horizontal rows as shown. Photograph shows correct color placement. Make four rows as shown.

2. Join flower rows to elephant rows with flower rows placed as shown in photograph.

3. For side flower borders, again join flower rows as shown, beginning with sashing squares at top and ending with sashing squares at bottom. Refer to photo for correct placement of sashing squares between flower rows. Join the flower/sashing borders to each side of quilt, matching corners.

4. Join 2¾" strips of fabric XIV together end to end. Cut two 100" long strips and add to sides of quilt. Trim if necessary.

5. Cut two 63½" long strips. Add remaining 2¾" squares of fabric XII to each end of border strips. Matching corners, join these strips to top and bottom of quilt.

Finishing

1. Quilt as desired. Make continuous binding by joining the nine 2½" strips of fabric XIV as you would for diagonal ends. Make 345" of binding. French-fold bind your quilt.

2. Have fun decorating the elephants. This might be a great time to include the child who will own the quilt. Use tassels, trim, and studs if desired.

Elephants on Parade

If you are able to find it, I feel that the grass outfield makes this quilt into a true miniature baseball field. If you live in a larger city and have a great quilt shop, finding the grass fabric should not be a problem. If you are in a smaller rural area, try the quilting catalogs. Although the other two greens used are dark, we kept them in the jewel tone family so they appear to be brighter. I wanted a texture for the glove, and a nice brown for the mounds and bats. This is an easy combination to put together.

Materials

▪ Fabric I	(medium green grass print)	4 yards

**For directional grass fabric, purchase ¼ yard additional fabric.*

▪ Fabric II	(dark green print)	2¼ yards
▫ Fabric III	(white on white checked print)	⅜ yard
▫ Fabric IV	(solid white)	2¾ yards
	(solid white for optional pillow)	⅜ yard
▪ Fabric V	(solid honey brown)	¾ yard
▪ Fabric VI	(medium brown texture print)	½ yard
▪ Fabric VII	(dark brown check)	½ yard
▪ Fabric VIII	(solid dark green)	1⅜ yards
▪ Fabric IX	(solid red)	⅛ yard
	(solid red for optional pillow)	½ yard
Backing		6 yards
Batting		85" x 108"
Appliqué film		scraps
Tear-away stabilizer		scraps
1" leather buttons for gloves		3

▪ Fabric pens or paints for lettering on dugouts, X's on baseballs, and baseball card name

▪ Large sheets of photo transfer paper to make 8" x 10" photos of your favorite player

▪ Polyester fiberfill for optional pillow

Home Run

79" x 101¾"
Designed by Dallas and Pam Bono.
Quilted by Faye Gooden.

Cutting

▪ *From Fabric I, cut: (medium green grass print)*

- Two 20¾"-wide strips. From this, cut:
  Two - 20¾" x 27⅞" (29b)

- One 23¾"-wide strip. From this, cut:
  Two - 16⅝" x 23¾" (23b)
  Two - 5¾" x 8⅜" (13) 8⅜" cut horizontally.
  Two - 3½" x 11⅜" (30)
  Three - 1⅝" x 3⅛" (A11c, B11c)

- One 11⅜"-wide strip. From this, cut:
  Two - 11⅜" x 17" (34)
  One - 2⅜" x 9½" (32)
  Four - 1¼" x 9½" (2)

- One 9⅛"-wide strip. From this, cut:
  Two - 9⅛" x 21⅛" (8)

- Two 7¼"-wide strips. From these, cut:
  One - 7¼" x 18⅞" (19)
  One - 7¼" x 20" (20)
  One - 2¾" x 6½" (18)
  Two - 7¼" x 9⅞" (11)
  Two - 7¼" squares (12a)
  One - 2⅜" x 6½" (17)

- Three 6½"-wide strips. From these, cut:
  Two - 6½" x 36⅞" (35) piece to = 73¼" long.
  Two - 5¾" squares (12b)
  Eight - 1⅝" square (1a)
  Three - 3⅞" squares (A12a, B12a)

- One 5"-wide strip. From this, cut:
  Six - 5" squares (C1a)

- One 3½"-wide strip. From this, cut:
  Eight - 3½" squares (3a)

- One 3⅛"-wide strip. From this, cut:
  Two - 3⅛" x 11¾" (5)
  Two - 3⅛" x 9½" (24)
  One - 2⅜" x 12⅞" (21)

- Two 2³⁄₄"-wide strips. From these, cut:
    Two - 2³⁄₄" x 20" (4)
    Twelve - 2³⁄₄" squares (1b, 6a, 15a)

- Two 1¹⁄₄"-wide strips. From these, cut:
    Three - 1¹⁄₄" x 3⁷⁄₈" (A9, B9)
    Three - 1¹⁄₄" x 3¹⁄₈" (A11a, B11a)
    Twenty-four - 1¹⁄₄" squares (A1a, B1a)

From Fabric II, cut: (dark green print)

- Two 20³⁄₄"-wide strips. From these, cut:
    Two - 20³⁄₄" x 27¹⁄₂" (29) piece to = 54¹⁄₂" long
    Two - 9¹⁄₂" x 19¹⁄₄" (26)
    Six - 5" squares (C1b)
    Two - 3¹⁄₂" squares (28a)
    Two - 1⁵⁄₈" squares (28b)

- Two 16⁵⁄₈"-wide strips. From this, cut:
    Two - 16⁵⁄₈" x 27¹⁄₂" (23) piece to = 54¹⁄₂" long
    One - 4⁵⁄₈" x 9¹⁄₂" (9)
    One - 4¹⁄₄" x 12¹⁄₂" (27)
    Two - 6⁷⁄₈" squares (8b)
    Two - 2³⁄₄" squares (34b)

From Fabric III, cut: (white on white-checked print)

- One 9¹⁄₂"-wide strip. From this, cut:
    Three - 9¹⁄₂" squares (C1)

From Fabric IV, cut: (solid white)

- Two 20³⁄₄"-wide strips. From this, cut:
    Two - 20³⁄₄"- x 23" (29a)
    One - 2¹⁄₂" x 8¹⁄₂" (baseball card)

- One 18⁷⁄₈"-wide strip. From this, cut:
    Two - 16⁵⁄₈" x 18⁷⁄₈" (23a)
    Two - 2³⁄₄"- x 17³⁄₈" (dugout signs)

- One 9¹⁄₂"-wide strip. From this, cut:
    Two - 9¹⁄₂" squares (3)
    Two - 9¹⁄₈" squares (8a)

- One 5"-wide strip. From this, cut:
    Two - 5" squares (34a)
    Two - 4¹⁄₂" squares (appliqué baseballs)
    One - 1¹⁄₄"- x 5" (41)
    Four - 1¹⁄₄" x 14" (39)
    Sixteen - 1¹⁄₄" squares (36a, 40a)

- One 2³⁄₄"-wide strip. From this cut:
    Six - 2³⁄₄"- squares (C1b)

- Ten 1⁵⁄₈"-wide strips for borders 42 and 43

From Fabric V, cut: (solid honey brown)

- One 5³⁄₄"-wide strip. From this, cut:
    One - 5³⁄₄"- x 12¹⁄₂" (28)

    One - 5" x 9¹⁄₂" (10)
    Two - 5" squares (13a)
    Two - 2³⁄₄"- x 5" (40)

- Two 5"-wide strips. From each strip, cut:
    One - 5" x 20³⁄₄" (36)
    Two - 5" x 9¹⁄₂" (1)

- Two 4¹⁄₄"-wide strips. From these, cut:
    One - 4¹⁄₄" x 17³⁄₄" (16 right)
    One - 4¹⁄₄" x 17" (16 left)
    Two - 4¹⁄₄" x 11³⁄₄" (7)
    Two - 3¹⁄₂" x 4⁵⁄₈" (37)

From Fabric VI, cut: (medium brown texture print)

- One 6¹⁄₈"-wide strip. From this, cut:
    Twelve - 2³⁄₄"- x 6¹⁄₈" (A1, B1)
    Three - 2³⁄₈" x 2³⁄₄" (A7, B7)
    Six - 1¹⁄₄" squares (A6a, B6a)

- One 3⁷⁄₈"--wide strip. From this, cut:
    Three - 3⁷⁄₈" x 6⁷⁄₈" (A12, B12)
    Three - 3¹⁄₈" x 3⁷⁄₈" (A11, B11)

- One 3¹⁄₂"-wide strip. From this, cut:
    Two - 3¹⁄₂" x 9⁷⁄₈" (38)
    Twelve - ⁷⁄₈" squares (A3a, B3a)
    Six - 2" x 2³⁄₈" (A2, B2, A4, B4)

- Two 1¹⁄₄"-wide strips. From this, cut:
    Six - 1¹⁄₄" x 9¹⁄₂" (A5, B5, A8, B8)

From Fabric VII, cut: (dark brown check)

- One 8³⁄₈"-wide strip. From this, cut:
    Two - 7¹⁄₄" x 8³⁄₈" (12)
    Three - 2³⁄₄" x 7⁵⁄₈" (A6, B6)
    Three - 2" x 5³⁄₄" (A3, B3)
    Three - 1⁵⁄₈" x 3⁷⁄₈" (A10, B10)
    Three - 1¹⁄₄" x 3¹⁄₈" (A11b, B11b)

- Two 2³⁄₄"-wide strips. From these, cut:
    One - 2³⁄₄" x 17³⁄₄" (15 right)
    One - 2³⁄₄" x 17" (15 left)
    Two - 2³⁄₄" x 11³⁄₄" (6)
    One - 2" x 16¹⁄₄" (14)

From Fabric VIII, cut: (solid dark green)

- Nine 2¹⁄₂"-wide strips for straight grain binding

- Nine 2"-wide strips for borders 44 and 45

From Fabric IX, cut: (solid red)

- Two 1¹⁄₂"-wide strips. From these, cut:
    Two - 1¹⁄₂" x 15¹⁄₂" (baseball card sides)
    Three - 1¹⁄₂" x 8¹⁄₂" (baseball card borders
        and dividers)

Assembly

Glove Blocks A and B

**Please note that block B (make 1) is mirror image of block A (make 2).
Refer to block drawings frequently when making the gloves.

1. Use diagonal corner technique (page 8) to make twelve of unit 1, three each of units 3 and 6, and three each of units 11 and 12. (One unit 11 and one unit 12 will be reversed for Block B.)

2. To make unit 11, join 11a, 11b, and 11c units together to form a tiny strip set. Position strip set on unit 11 as shown, right sides together and stitch as you would for any diagonal corner. Trim seam and press. For mirror image, reverse positions.

Unit 11

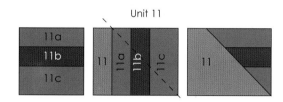

3. Join units 9, 10, 11, and 12 in a row as shown and set aside.

4. Join four of unit 1 in a row as shown. Join units 2, 3, and 4 in a horizontal row. Join to bottom of combined unit 1; then add unit 5 to bottom of combined units 2-4.

5. Join units 6 and 7; then add unit 8 to bottom of combined units. Join these to bottom of glove as shown; then add combined units 9-12 to appropriate side for A and B blocks.

Base Block C

1. Begin by using diagonal corner technique to make two of unit 1b. Refer to block C illustration and be sure that the diagonal corner units you are making are mirror images.

Base Block, make 3

2. Refer to illustration of making baseline for block C and place diagonal corners on unit 1, right sides together as shown. Join as you would for any diagonal corner. Trim seams and press outwards. Continue to add diagonal corners 1a to complete the base block. Make 3 for units 25 and 33.

Baseline for Block C

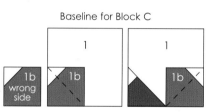

Glove Block A - Make 2

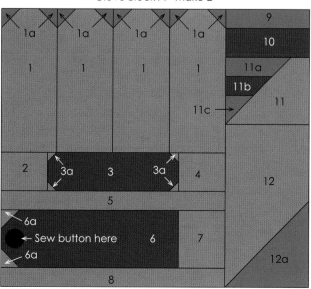

Glove Block B- Make 1

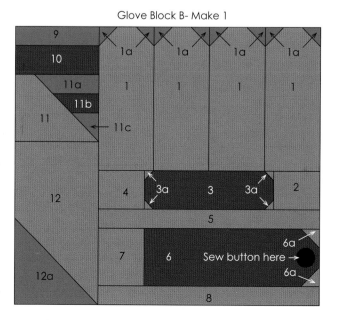

Baseball Card for Quilt and Optional Pillow

**The cutting instructions given are for the quilt only. Should you choose to make a pillow also, double the number of cuts from fabrics IV and IX. For the pillow, you will need one 10½" x 15½" piece of backing. Instructions are given for one baseball card.

Baseball Card

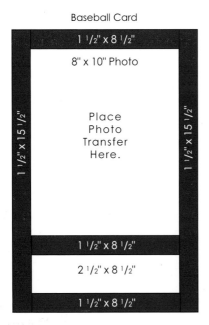

1½" x 8½"

8" x 10" Photo

1½" x 15½"   Place Photo Transfer Here.   1½" x 15½"

1½" x 8½"

2½" x 8½"

1½" x 8½"

1. Follow manufacturer's instructions for use of photo transfer paper, and enlarge a snapshot of your favorite player to 8" x 10". Transfer photo to white or muslin fabric. Cut out, leaving ¼" seam allowance around entire photo.

2. Join 1½" x 8½" strips of fabric IX to top and bottom of photo. Join one 2½" x 8½" piece of fabric IV to one more 1½" x 8½" strip of fabric IX. Add these to bottom of card.

3. Join 1½" x 15½" strips of fabric IX to opposite sides of baseball card, framing it.

4. Using fabric paint or pen, print the name of your favorite player in the white panel. Allow proper drying time. You might want to include batting average and date under the name in the label with black, fine-tip pen.

5. Press under ¼" around baseball card. Card will later be appliquéd or top-stitched onto quilt top as shown in quilt assembly diagram.

6. Make pillow in same manner, and quilt if desired. Place backing right sides together on top of baseball card front and stitch around card, leaving at least a 4" wide opening at the bottom.

7. Clip corners, and turn pillow right side out. Stuff with fiberfill and hand stitch opening closed.

Baseball Bat

1. Refer to quilt assembly diagram for position and numbering of baseball bats. Use diagonal corner technique to make two each of units 36 and 40.

2. To assemble bat portion of quilt, begin by joining units 37 and 38 for each bat. Join unit 39 to opposite long sides of these combined units; then add unit 36 to right side of bat, and unit 40 to left side.

3. Turn bats so that the handles face each other as shown and join unit 41 between bats.

4. Join the 1⅝" wide strips of fabric IV end to end. Cut three 73¼" long strips which now become unit 42. Join unit 42 to opposite long sides of bats. Third 73¼" strip will be added to bottom of quilt top later. Set it aside along with bats.

Bottom Section

1. To assemble the quilt top, refer frequently to our quilt assembly diagram. To assemble the quilt top, begin with the two bullpens. Use diagonal corner technique to make two each of units 3 and 6, and four each of unit 1.

2. Refer to diagram and join units 1, 2, 3, 2, and 1 in a vertical row. Make two. Join unit 4 to sides (keeping in mind that dugouts are mirror images), then add unit 5 to bottom. Join units 6 and 7; then add them to the bottom of the bullpen. Using a red fabric pen, draw all X's on baseballs as shown.

3. Use diagonal corner technique to make two mirror image unit 8. Add diagonal corner 8a first. Trim seam and press; then add diagonal corner 8b. Use diagonal corner technique to make two each of mirror image units 12, 13, and 15.

4. For center bottom section of quilt, join units 9 and 10. Refer to diagram for correct placement of mirror image unit 8. Join to opposite sides of combined 9-10 units. Join two mirror image units 13 as shown; then add unit 14 to bottom. Join mirror image units 12 to opposite short sides of combined units 13-14 as shown; then add unit 11 to opposite short sides. Join the 8-10 row to the 11-14 row, matching base line with home plate.

5. Join mirror image units 15 and 16 as shown. For left (visiting team) dugout, join unit 17 to right side; then add unit 19 to top of the 15-17 combined units. For right (home team) dugout, join unit 18 to left side as shown; then add Unit 20 to top.

Quilt Construction

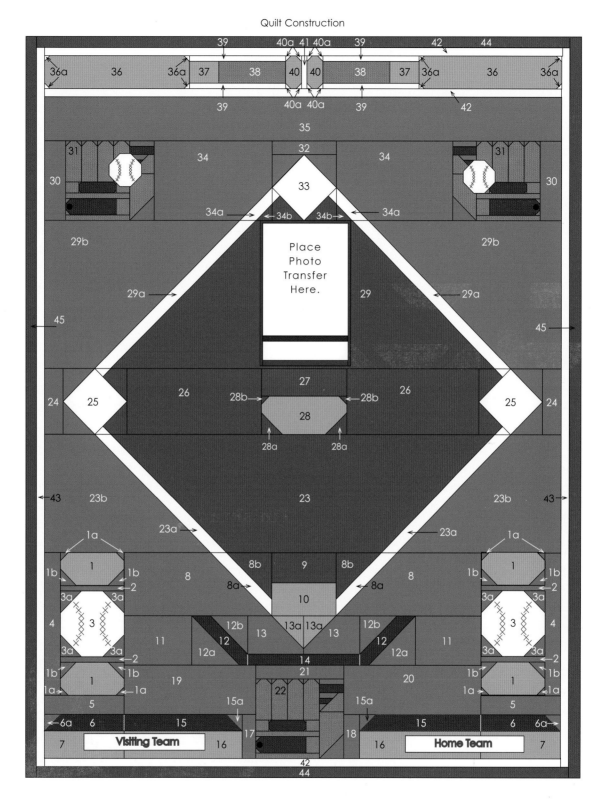

6. Join unit 21 to block A, Unit 22 as shown. Join the visiting team dugout to the left side of the glove section, and the home team dugout to the right side of the glove section. Join this now completed bottom section to the two rows previously joined.

7. To complete bottom section of quilt, join the bullpen sections to opposite sides of the dugout/glove section, referring to illustration for correct placement of each bullpen. Match dugout seams.

8. Using fabric paint, write the name of your child's home team and favorite visiting team on the dugout signs. Allow to dry for 24 hours. When dry, press appliqué film to back of dugout signs and press them on dugouts. Satin stitch in place.

Center Section

1. Use diagonal corner technique to make one of unit 28. Join units 27 and 28 as shown; then add unit 26 to opposite sides of these combined units. Turn base blocks C (unit 25) in positions shown on quilt assembly diagram and join them to opposite ends of the 26-28 combined units; then add unit 24 to opposite sides.

2. Use diagonal end technique (page 10) to make one each of units 23 and 29. Refer to illustration of unit 23 assembly for correct position of each diagonal end. Assemble Unit 29 in the same manner.

Units 23 and 29

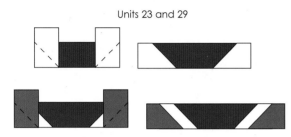

3. Join completed unit 23 to bottom of pitcher's mound center section matching base lines carefully. Join completed unit 29 to top of this section as shown, matching base lines.

Top Section

1. Lay 2nd base (unit 33) in correct position as shown in illustration. Join unit 32 to top of 2nd base. Use diagonal corner technique to make two mirror image units 34. Refer to diagram for correct placement of diagonal corners. Add corners in alphabetical order. Join mirror image units 34 to opposite sides of 2nd base section, matching base lines carefully.

2. Join glove blocks A & B (unit 31) to unit 30, referring to illustration for correct placement of mirror image glove blocks. Join gloves to opposite ends of 2nd base section.

3. Join the two 6½" x 36⅞" pieces of fabric I for unit 35. Join unit 35 to top of 2nd base/glove section. Join this completed section to the top of center section, matching base lines.

4. Join completed bats to top of Unit 35.

Quilt Top Assembly

1. Join top and bottom sections together; then add remaining unit 42 to bottom of quilt top.

2. Center baseball card as shown in infield and pin or baste in place. Hand appliqué around outside of card, or top-stitch card in place along edge with red thread. You

may also want to secure it further by top stitching around white space with name.

3. Cut remainder of 1⅝" wide strip of fabric IV into two 99" long strips and join to sides of quilt top. Trim off any excess.

4. Join 2"-wide strips of fabric VIII end to end. Cut two 76" long strips and join to top and bottom of quilt, trimming off any excess.

5. Cut remainder of 2" wide strip into two 102" long strips. Join to sides of quilt and trim off any excess.

6. Cut out baseballs as directed on illustration, cutting off corners. Using a red fabric pen, draw X's on baseballs. Press appliqué film to back of baseballs using our technique described on page 11. Press baseballs onto glove units 31 as shown and satin stitch around baseballs with white thread.

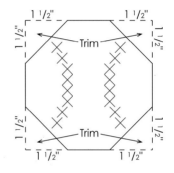

Finishing

1. Quilt as desired. As there are very large open areas, we stippled the infield and outfield grass and stitched the patchwork in the ditch. We suggest quilting around ballplayer's face on baseball card to add stability.

2. Make 170" of straight-grain binding from fabric VIII and bind quilt.

3. Sew buttons on gloves.

Home Run

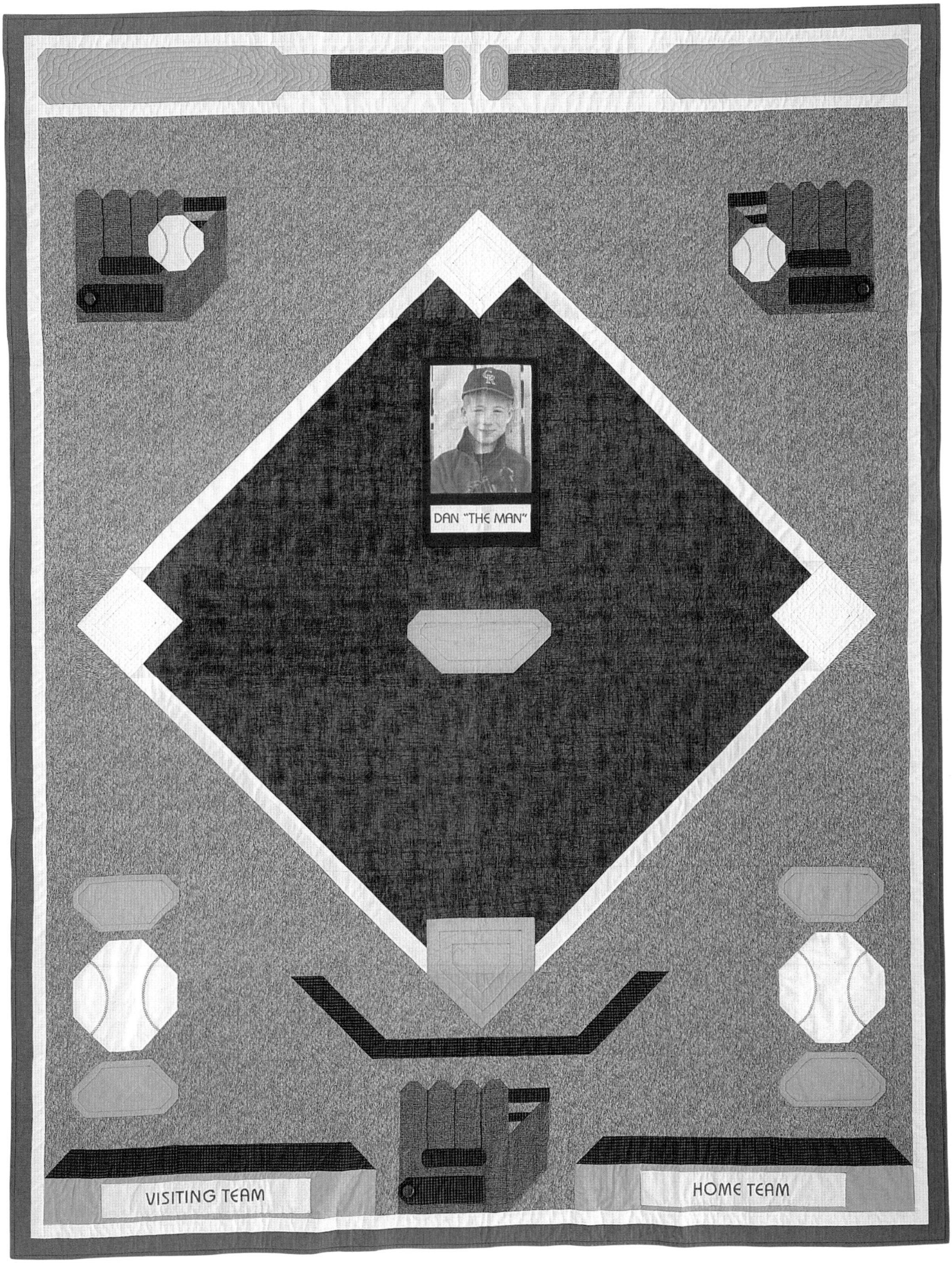

DAN "THE MAN"

VISITING TEAM

HOME TEAM

The bright peach print we found accentuates our mischevious black, white, and gray cat. If you look closely, you may find a cute blue water print for the fishbowl and outer borders. A dark navy batik frames each block and enhances the fishbowls. Choose a bright orange, flowery print and a light peach print for the goldfish.

Materials

☐	Fabric I	(white-on-white print)	³/₈ yard
■	Fabric II	(solid black)	¹/₄ yard
▧	Fabric III	(medium gray print)	¹/₈ yard
▨	Fabric IV	(light gray solid)	¹/₄ yard
▨	Fabric V	(bright peach print)	⁵/₈ yard
▨	Fabric VI	(blue water print)	2 yards
▨	Fabric VII	(dark olive print)	⁵/₈ yard
■	Fabric VIII	(navy print)	1¹/₈ yard
▨	Fabric IX	(dark orange print)	¹/₂ yard
▨	Fabric X	(light peach print)	³/₈ yard
	Backing		3³/₄ yards
	Batting		66" x 66"
	Appliqué film		1¹/₂ yards
	Tear-away stabilizer		1 yard
	Black fabric pen		

Midnight Snack

60" square
Finished block sizes: 14" square
Designed by Mindy Kettner.
Quilted by Faye Gooden.

Cutting

☐ *From Fabric I, cut: (white-on-white print)*

- Three 2¹/₂" -wide strips. From these, cut:
  Five – 2¹/₂" x 12¹/₂" (B2)
  Four – 2¹/₂" x 4¹/₂" (A14)
  Twelve – 2¹/₂" squares (A18, A20)
  Four – 1¹/₂" x 2¹/₂" (A3)

- One 1¹/₂"-wide strip. From this, cut:
  Eight – 1¹/₂" squares (A19b)
  Scrap for six whites of eyes

■ *From Fabric II, cut: (solid black)*

- Three 1¹/₂" -wide strips. From these, cut:
  Eight – 1¹/₂" x 5¹/₂" (A16)
  Eight – 1¹/₂" x 3¹/₂" (A13)
  Eight – 1¹/₂" x 2¹/₂" (A5, A10a)
  Scrap for four noses

▧ *From Fabric III, cut: (medium gray print)*

- One 2¹/₂"-wide strip. From this, cut:
  Eight – 2¹/₂" squares (A15)

- One 1¹/₂" wide strip. From this, cut:
  Twenty-four – 1¹/₂" squares (A12a, A13a, A19a)

▨ *From Fabric IV, cut: (light gray solid)*

- One 3¹/₂"-wide strip. From this, cut:
  Four – 3¹/₂" x 6¹/₂" (A12)
  Six – 2¹/₂" x 3¹/₂" (A9, A10)

- One 2¹/₂"-wide strip. From this, cut:
  Ten – 2¹/₂" x 3¹/₂" (A10, A19)
  Four – 1¹/₂" x 2¹/₂" (A8)

▨ *From Fabric V, cut: (bright peach print)*

- One 6¹/₂"-wide strip. From this, cut:
  Eight – 4¹/₂" x 6¹/₂" (A11)

- Three 2½" wide strips. From these, cut:
  Eight – 2½" x 5½" (A17)
  Sixteen – 2½" squares (A1, A7, A9a)
  Sixteen – 1½" x 2½" (A2, A10b, A21)
  Four – 1½" x 3½" (A4)

- Three 1½"-wide strip. From this, cut:
  Twenty-eight – 1½" squares (A6, A16a, A20a)
  Four – 1½" x 14½" (A22)

From Fabric VI, cut: (blue water print)

- Four 7½"-wide strips. From these, cut:
  One – 7½" x 23½" from each of the four strips.
  Sew two of the 23½" pieces together to equal
  7½" x 46½" for border 1; make 2.

- Three 7½"-wide strips. Combine these strips and cut
  to equal two 60½" strips for border 2.

- Two 7½"-wide strips. From these, cut:
  Five – 7½" x 12½" (B1)

From Fabric VII, cut: (dark olive print)

- Two 2½"-wide strips. From these, cut:
  Twenty – 2½" squares (B1a, B2a)
  Twenty – 1½" x 2½" (B4, B6)

- Eight 1½"-wide strips. From these, cut:
  Ten – 1½" x 14½" (B8)
  Ten – 1½" x 12½" (B7)
  Twenty – 1½" squares (B3a)

From Fabric VIII, cut: (navy print)

- Eight 2½"-wide strips. Six strips for straight grain binding.
  From remainder, cut:
  Five – 2½" x 10½" (B3)
  Three – 1½" x 8½" (B5)

- Ten 1½" wide strips. Join seven strips together end to end
  for sashing 2 and 3. From remainder, cut:
  Six – 1½" x 14½" (sashing 1)
  Two – 1½" x 8½" (B5)
  Cut one 8½" piece from each strip so you will have
  enough fabric for two 14½" cuts from each strip.

From Fabric IX, cut: (dark orange print)

- Three 4½"-wide strips. From these, cut:
  Ten – 4½" x 10½" (appliqué fish)

From Fabric X, cut: (light peach print)

- Two 4½"-wide strips. From these, cut:
  Seven – 4½" x 10½" (appliqué fish)

Assembly

Block A

Please note that units 4-10 are reversed to make two blocks with right-facing tails, and two blocks with left facing tails.

Block A

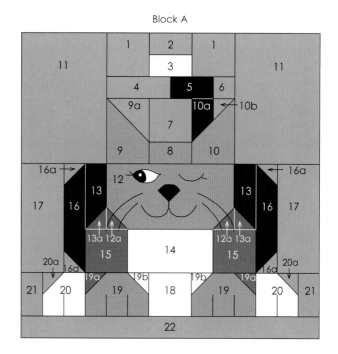

1. Begin by using diagonal corner technique on page 8 to make one each of units 9, 10, 12, 13, 16, 19, and 20. Refer to the illustration for block A frequently for correct mirror image placement of diagonal corners.

2. To make unit 10, refer to unit 10 construction diagram and begin by joining units 10a and 10b together as shown. This combined unit now becomes your diagonal corner. Place it on unit 10 as shown and stitch as for any diagonal corner. Trim seam and press. Reverse for mirror image.

Unit 10 construction—reverse for mirror image

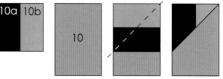

Unit 10 mirror image

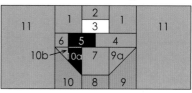

3. To assemble block, join units 2 and 3, then add unit 1 to opposite sides of combined units. Join units 4, 5, and 6 in a row, then join to combined units 1-3. Join units 7 and 8. Join units 9 and 10 to opposite sides of units 7-8, referring to photograph for correct placement of mirror image tail units. Join unit 11 to opposite sides of tail section to complete top of cat.

4. For cat bottom, begin by joining units 13, 12, and 13 in a row as shown, referring to diagram for correct placement of mirror-image unit 13. Join units 15, 14, and 15 in a horizontal row as shown, then add this row to bottom of face section. Join mirror image unit 16 to unit 17 as shown. Join these combined units to opposite sides of cat face section. Refer to diagram to join units 21, 20, 19, 18, 19, 20, and 21 in a horizontal row as shown. Be careful to place mirror-image units correctly. Add this row to bottom of combined units 12-17, then add unit 22 to bottom to complete cat bottom section.

5. Join the top and bottom cat sections, matching seams carefully.

6. Trace a face onto each cat, checking quilt photograph for correct positioning of eyes. Each cat is looking at the center fish! Follow manufacturer's instructions and draw eyes and nose onto wrong side of appliqué film. Press eyes and nose in place on each cat, and draw remainder of face with a black fabric pen.

7. Make four of block A as directed.

Block B

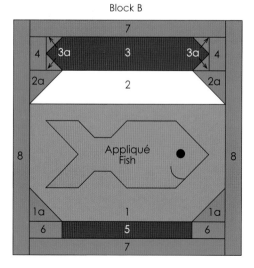

Block B

1. Use diagonal corner technique to make one each of units 1, 2, and 3.

2. Join units 1 and 2. Join units 4, 3, and 4 in a row as shown, then add this row to top of unit 2. Join units 6, 5, and 6 in a horizontal row as shown, then add this row to bottom of unit 1. Join unit 7 to top and bottom of fishbowl, then join unit 8 to opposite sides.

3. Refer to quilt photo for correct placement and colors of fish. Trace fish onto appliqué film and cut out. Press fish in place, centered in fishbowls. Three will be facing left, and two will be facing right. Satin stitch in place. Draw faces on fish with black fabric pen.

4. Make five fishbowl blocks.

Quilt Top Assembly

1. Join sashing 1 strips between the A and B blocks to create three horizontal rows as shown.

2. Join sashing 2 strips together end to end. Cut four $44\frac{1}{2}$" strips for sashing 2, and two $46\frac{1}{2}$" strips for sashing 3.

3. Join the rows together with vertical sashing 2 strips between each horizontal row and at top and bottom of joined block rows as shown. Trim excess.

4. Join sashing 3 to opposite sides of quilt top. Trim excess.

5. Join the two $46\frac{1}{2}$" border strips to sides of quilt top as shown.

6. Join the two $60\frac{1}{2}$" border strips to top and bottom of quilt top.

7. Use pattern for fish to trace twelve remaining fish onto appliqué film. Referring to quilt photo, press fish into place using measurements shown on Border Appliqué illustration. Satin stitch in place, and draw faces with black fabric pen.

Finishing

1. Quilt as desired. We used an echo stitch around each cat and stitched in the ditch around all the patchwork and fish, then quilted large waves on the large outer borders.

2. Make 250" of straight-grain binding from fabric VIII and bind quilt.

Border Appliqué Placement

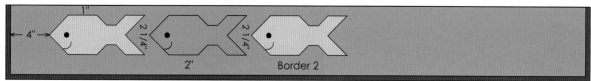

Midnight Snack

Cat Face
(top)

Fish

Cat Face
(left)

Cat eyes
(bottom)

Cat Face
(right)

My Carousel

FABRIC TIPS ▶

Fabric Tips: Since the horse is the focal point it must contrast significantly with the pink background. We used two shades of gray plus black, to give the mane a flowing look. The dark burgundy print and decorative appliqués accentuate the canopy and scallops. The plaid adds a sporty look and balance. Have fun with the trim. Very few carousel horses are under-dressed!

Materials

■ Fabric I	(dusty rose print)	$2^5/8$ yards
■ Fabric II	(burgundy or grape print)	4 yards
■ Fabric III	(gold/pink/green plaid)	$1^3/4$ yards
□ Fabric IV	(white-on-white print)	$5/8$ yard
■ Fabric V	(gold print)	$3/4$ yard
■ Fabric VI	(black print)	$1/4$ yard
■ Fabric VII	(medium gray print)	$1/4$ yard
■ Fabric VIII	(dark gray print)	$1/4$ yard
Backing		$5^1/2$ yards
Batting		86" x 100"
Appliqué film		$1/2$ yard
Tear-away stabilizer		1 yard
$1/4$"-wide gold braided trim for reins		$3/4$ yard
$1/2$"-wide flat, white lace with gold metallic accents		$5^1/4$ yards
$7/8$" decorative gold buttons		5
$1/2$" decorative gold buttons		15

My Carousel

Quilt finished size without scallops: 60" x 84"
Quilt finished size with scallops: 80" x 94"
Designed by Pam and Robert Bono.
Quilted by Faye Gooden.

Cutting

■ *From Fabric I, cut: (dusty rose print)*

- One 22"-wide strip. From this, cut:
  One - 17" x 22" (HT1)
  One - 17" x $21^3/4$" (HT3)

- Cut remaining piece into one $5^3/4$" x 22" piece. From this, cut:
  One - 6" x $11^3/4$" (HB15)
  One - $5^1/2$" x 8" (HB38)

- From remaining scrap, cut:
  Eight - 2" squares (HT20a, HT33a, HT50, HT55a, HT64a, HT71b, HT81b, HB30a)

- One $18^1/4$"-wide strip. From this, cut:
  One - $15^1/2$" x $18^1/4$" (HT66)
  One - $13^1/4$" x $16^1/2$" (HB20)
  One - $4^1/4$" x $13^1/4$" (HB39)
  One - $2^1/2$" x $13^1/4$" (HT67)
  One – $4^1/4$" square (HB37)
  Three - $1^3/4$" squares (HB21b, HB34a)
  One - $1^1/4$" x $3^1/4$" (HB28)
  Four - $1^1/4$" x $2^3/4$" (HT31, HT78, HB5, HB14)
  Eleven - $1^1/4$" squares (HT11a, HT12, HT13a, HT22a, HT59a, HB6a, HB7, HB16a, HB32b, HB35a)

- One $17^3/4$"-wide strip. From this, cut:
  Two - $7^3/4$" x $17^3/4$" (C8a)
  Two - $8^5/8$" x $17^3/8$" (C5, C6) Cut as shown in Diagram 1.
  One - $4^1/4$" x 17" (HT 61)
  Two - $2^1/2$" x $16^1/2$" (C7)

Diagram 1

- One 5¼"-wide strip. From this, cut:
    One - 5¼" x 24½" (HT58)
    Three - 4¼" x 5" (HT28, HT40, HT54)
    Two - 2" x 5" (HT38, HT79)
- Four 5"-wide strips. From this, cut:
    Four - 5" x 29" (long side borders to be pieced)
    One - 5" x 5¾" (HB10)
    One - 2¾" x 5" (HT15)
    One - 1¼" x 5" (HB4)
    One - 4¼" x 8¾" (HT4)
    Two - 3½" x 4¼" (HT69a, HT76)
    Three - 2¾" x 4¼" (HT24, HT43, HB12)
    Three - 2" x 4¼" (HT5, HT29, HB32a)
    One - 4" x 7¼" (HB25)
    One - 1¾" x 2¾" (HB31)
    One - 1¼" x 3½" (HT30)
- One 3½"-wide strip. From this, cut:
    Two - 3½" squares (HT68a, HT69b)
    Two - 2" x 3½" (HT23, HB17)
    One - 3" x 4¼" (HT60)
    One - 2¾" square (HT8)
    Two - 2" x 2¾" (HT57, HB33)
    One - 2" x 3" (HB3)
    One - 2" x 5¾" (HB1)
    One - 1¼" x 8¾" (HB19)
    One - 1¼" x 2" (HB36)

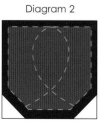 *From Fabric II, cut: (burgundy or grape print)*

- One 7¾"-wide strip. From this, cut:
    One - 7¾" x 40¾" (C8)

- One 8⅝"-wide strip. From this, cut:
    Two - 8⅝" x 17⅜" (C3, C4, C5, C6) Cut into
    triangles as shown in Diagram 1 on page 57.
    One - 5¾" x 6½" (HT63)
    One - 1¼" x 5¾" (HT18)
    One - 1¼" x 4¼" (HT21)

- Three 8½"-wide strips. From this, cut:
    Two - 8½" x 16½" (C1)
    Eight - 8½" squares for canopy scallops. Cut bottom
    corners as shown in Diagram 2.
    One - 3½" x 5" (HT81)
    Four - 2¾" squares (HT33, HT41, HT44a, HT84b)
    Cut third strip into three 2¼"-wide strips.
From these, cut:
    Fifteen - 2¼" x 3" (decorations for horse and floor)
    Cut corners as shown in Diagram 3.

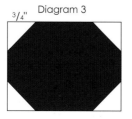

Diagram 2

2⅛"

Diagram 3

¾"

- From scraps, cut:
    One - 2" square (HT20b)
    Three 1¼" x 2" (HT7, H19, H30a)

- Five 6½"-wide strips. From these, cut:
    Nineteen - 6½" x 10½" (outer scallops) Cut bottom
    corners as shown in Diagram 4.
    One - 1¼" x 2¾" (HT16)
    One - 1¼" square (HT17a)

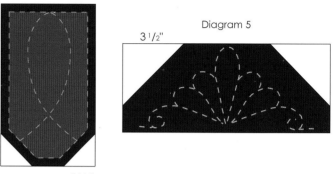

Diagram 4

2½"

Diagram 5

3½"

- One 5"-wide strip. From this, cut:
    Two - 5" x 12" (pillar bases) Cut corners as shown in
    Diagram 5.
- Use 1⅓ yards to make continuous 2½"-wide
bias binding.

▨ *From Fabric III, cut: (gold/pink/green plaid)*

- One 8⅝"-wide strip. From this, cut:
    Two - 8⅝" x 17⅜" (C3, C4) See Diagram 1 page 57 for
    correct cutting.
    One - 4¼" x 7¼" (HT44)
    Three - 2" squares (HT45a, HT50, HT89a)

- Two 8½"-wide strips. From these, cut:
    One - 8½" x 16½" (C2)
    Six - 8½" squares (canopy scallops) Cut bottom
    corners as shown in Diagram 2.
    One - 4¼" x 5" (HT84)
    One - 3½" x 4¼" (HT47)

- Five 6½"-wide strips. From these, cut:
    Nineteen - 6½" x 10½" (outer scallops) Cut bottom
    corners as shown in Diagram 3.
    One - 2¾" x 3½" (HT83)
    One - 1¼" x 3½" (HT74)
    One - 2" x 2¾" (HT82)
    One - 2" x 4¼" (HT48)

☐ *From Fabric IV, cut: (white-on-white print)*

- One 5"-wide strip. From this, cut:
    One - 5" x 7¼" (HT39)
    One - 5" x 5¾" (HT89)
    One - 3½" x 5" (HT80)
    Two - 2¾" x 5" (HT17, HT20)
    One - 4¼" x 6½" (HT64)
    One - 4¼" square (HT26a)

One - 2" x 8³⁄₄" (HB32)
One - 2" x 7¹⁄₄" (HT45)

- One 3¹⁄₂"-wide strip. From this, cut:
    One - 3¹⁄₂" x 11³⁄₄" (HT52)
    One - 3¹⁄₂" x 5³⁄₄" (HB21)
    One - 3¹⁄₂" square (HT76a)
    One - 2³⁄₄" x 11" (HT42)
    One - 2³⁄₄" x 10¹⁄₄" (HB16)

- One 2³⁄₄"-wide strip. From this, cut:
    Two - 2³⁄₄" x 4¹⁄₄" (HT22, HT27)
    Two - 2³⁄₄" x 3¹⁄₂" (HT73, HB29)
    Three - 2³⁄₄" squares (HT10, HT34a, HT71a)
    Three - 2" x 3¹⁄₂" (HT46, HT48a, HT49)

- One 2"-wide strip. From this, cut:
    One - 2" x 4¹⁄₄" (HT37)
    Three - 2" x 2³⁄₄" (HT36, HT82a, HB22)
    Seven - 2" squares (HT32a, HT44b, HT84a, HT88, HB12a, HB20a)
    Nine - 1¹⁄₄" squares (HT20c, HT34b, HT35a, HT37a, HT81a, HT85a, HB10a, HB24a)
- One 1¹⁄₄"-wide strip. From this, cut:
    Two - 1¹⁄₄" x 3¹⁄₂" (HT90, HB18)
    Three - 1¹⁄₄" x 2" (HT19a, HT86, HB26)
    One - 1¹⁄₄" x 5³⁄₄" (HB19a, HB23)
    Two - 1¹⁄₄" x 2³⁄₄" (HB11, HB13)

From Fabric V, cut: (gold print)

- One 14"-wide strip. From this, cut:
    One - 14" x 29". Cut this piece into four 3¹⁄₂" x 29" strips for outer poles.

- From remainder, cut:
    One - 8⁷⁄₈" square (quilt corners) cut in half diagonally to yield two triangles.

- Two 4¹⁄₄"-wide strips. From this, cut:
    Two - 4¹⁄₄" x 30¹⁄₂" (floor to be pieced)
    One - 2³⁄₄" x 6¹⁄₂" (HT65)

- One 2³⁄₄"-wide strip. From this, cut:
    Two - 2³⁄₄" x 17" (HT2, HT62)

From Fabric VI, cut: (black print)

- One 3¹⁄₂"-wide strip. From this, cut:
    One - 3¹⁄₂" x 8" (HT69)
    One - 3¹⁄₂" x 4¹⁄₄" (HT32)
    One - 3¹⁄₂" square (HT4a)
    One - 2³⁄₄" x 3¹⁄₂" (HT34)
    One - 2" x 3¹⁄₂" (HB35)
    One - 2³⁄₄" square (HT11)
    One - 2" x 5³⁄₄" (HT70)
    Six - 2" squares (HT5b, HT14, HT25b, HT26b, HT76b, HB37a)

- One 1³⁄₄"-wide strip. From this, cut:
    One - 1³⁄₄" x 5³⁄₄" (HB34)
    One - 1¹⁄₂" square (HB37b)

One - 1¹⁄₄" x 2³⁄₄" (HT35)
Four - 1¹⁄₄" x 2" (HT6, HT31a, HT77)
One - 1¹⁄₄" x 3¹⁄₂" (HT72)
Four - 1¹⁄₄" squares (HT7a, HT13, HT16a, HT73a)
One - ³⁄₄" square cut in half diagonally for eye and nose.

From Fabric VII, cut: (medium grey print)

- One 3¹⁄₂"-wide strip. From this, cut:
    One - 3¹⁄₂" x 4" (HB21a)
    One - 3¹⁄₂" square (HB15a)
    One - 2" x 3¹⁄₂" (HT53)
    One - 2³⁄₄" x 4¹⁄₄" (HT59)
    Two - 2³⁄₄" squares (HT56, HB6)
    Two - 2" x 2³⁄₄" (HB2, HB30)
    One - 2¹⁄₄" square (HB20b)

- One 2"-wide strip. From this, cut:
    One - 2" x 5³⁄₄" (HB24)
    Two - 2" x 4¹⁄₄" (HT25, HT55)
    Five - 2" squares (HT89b, HB9, HB22a, HB25a, HB29a)
    Three - 1¹⁄₄" x 2" (HT51, HT91, HB27)
    Three - 1¹⁄₄" squares (HB4a, HB8, HB25b)

From Fabric VIII, cut: (dark grey print)

- One 5"-wide strip. From this, cut:
    One - 5" square (HT68)
    One - 2" x 5" (HT5a)
    One - 4¹⁄₄" x 6¹⁄₂" (HT26)
    One - 4¹⁄₄" square (HT71)
    Two - 2³⁄₄" x 4¹⁄₄" (HT9, HT75)
    One - 3¹⁄₂" square (HT69c)
    One - 2" x 5" (HT70a)
    Four - 2" squares (HT25a, HT37a, HT83a, HT85)
    One - 1¹⁄₄" x 2" (HT87)
    Six - 1¹⁄₄"-squares (HT10a, HT36a, HT72a, HT88a)

Assembly

The quilt is divided into three main sections: canopy (C) 23¹⁄₄" x 60", horse top (HT) 44¹⁄₄" x 45", and horse bottom (HB) 12³⁄₄" x 45". Assembly begins with the canopy section.

Canopy (C)

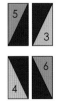

1. Referring to illustration of canopy top and illustration for joining cut triangles, stitch units 3, 4, 5, and 6 together as shown. Press out and trim off tips.

2. Using diagonal end technique on page 10, join units 8 and 8a as shown in illustration for canopy top.

3. Refer once again to canopy illustration and join units 1-7 together in a row as shown. Matching seams, join unit 8 to top of these joined units.

Canopy

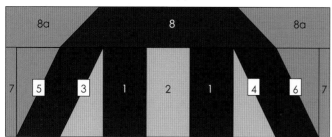

Adding Scallops

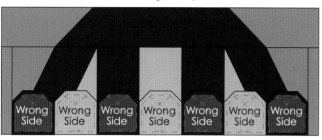

4. Refer to Diagram 2 on page 58 to draw the quilting design onto right side of four pieces of fabric II and of three pieces of fabric III.

5. Using one piece of fabric II or III cut for canopy scallops as a pattern, cut seven pieces of thin batting. To make scallops, place two pieces of like-colored fabric scallops, right sides together, and place cut batting under the two pieces. Stitch around three sides through all thicknesses as shown. Secure ends and clip corners. Turn right side out so that batting is sandwiched between the fabric scallops, then press. Repeat for each scallop.

6. You may quilt scallops on marked lines or you may satin stitch them. We worked a narrow satin stitch with metallic gold thread on the darker fabric and a burgundy satin stitch on the plaid scallops. Referring to photograph, sew a 7/8" button on all fabric II scallops as shown in photo on page 65.

7. Place scallops as shown in canopy top illustration with right sides of scallops facing right side of pieced canopy top. Pin in place with edges touching. Baste 1/8" from raw edge as shown.

Horse Top

We suggest marking each completed section with the section number to avoid confusion when joining sections to complete the horse top.

1. Join units 1, 2, and 3 together in a row as shown to complete section A.

Section A

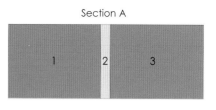

2. For section B, use diagonal corner technique to make one each of units 4, 7, and 10. Use diagonal end technique on page 10 to make one of unit 5, then add diagonal corner 5b. To assemble section B, join units 6 and 7 together as shown, then add unit 5 to left side. Join unit 4 to top of these joined units. Join units 8, 9, and 10 in a row and join this row toother combined units, matching seams.

Section B

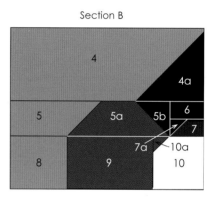

3. To prepare units for section C, begin by placing unit 13 and unit 13a right sides together. Stitch diagonally across center and trim seam. Open out and press. Use diagonal corner technique to make one each of units 11, 16, 17, 20, and 22. For unit 20, join each diagonal corner in alphabetical order. After joining diagonal corner 20b, trim seam and press out, then add diagonal corner 20c. Use diagonal end technique to make one of unit 19.

Section C

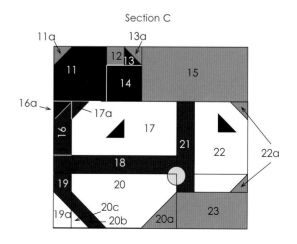

4. To assemble section C, join units 12 and 13 as shown. Add unit 14 to bottom of combined units. Join unit 11 to left side of this row and unit 15 to right side. Join units 16 and 17, then add unit 18 to bottom. Join units 19 and 20, matching seams. Add these combined units to combined units 16-18 as shown. Join units 21 and 22, then add unit 23 to bottom. Join combined units 21 22, and 23 to right side of combined units 16-20, matching seams. Add combined units 11-15 to top. Trace a ¾" triangle for eye onto appliqué film. Repeat for nose. Press these onto back side of solid black scrap according to manufacturer's instructions. Referring to illustration, press eye in place on unit 17, and nose in place on unit 22. Draw mouth with water-erasable

pen. Place tear-away stabilizer under eye, nose and mouth, and satin stitch around eye and nose, then satin stitch mouth with black thread.

5. Use diagonal corner technique to make one each of units 25 and 26 for section D. To complete section, join units 24-28 in a horizontal row as shown.

Section D

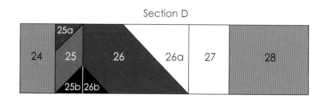

Horse Top

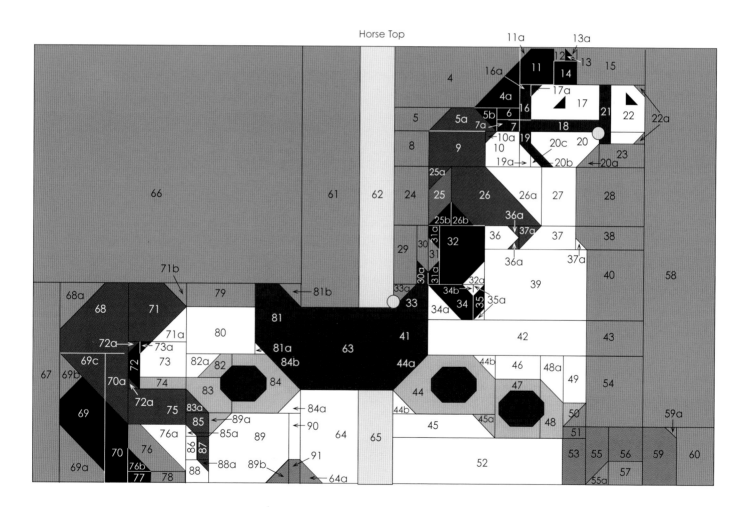

6. For section E, use diagonal corner technique to make one each of units 32, 33, 34, and 35. Use diagonal end technique to make one each of units 30 and 31.

7. Join units 29-32 in a row as shown, matching seams. Join units 33-35 in a row. Join the two rows, matching seams.

8. For section F, use diagonal corner technique to make one each of units 36, 37, and 38. Upon completion, join the units together in a row as shown. Join units 39 and 40, then stitch the two rows together, once again matching seams.

9. To complete section G, join units 41, 42, and 43 together in a row as shown.

10. To piece section H, use diagonal corner technique to make one each of units 44 and 45. To make unit 50, place 2" squares of fabrics I and III right sides together. Stitch diagonally down center. Trim seam and press out. Use diagonal end technique to make one of unit 48.

11. To assemble section H, begin by joining units 44 and 45 as shown. Join units 46 and 47, then add unit 48 to right side, matching seams. Join units 49, 50 and 51 in a vertical row and join this row to right side of combined units 46-48. Join combined units 44-45 to left side. Join units 52 and 53, then add this to other combined units.

12. On appliqué film, trace around outer edge of $2^{1}/4$"x 3" piece of fabric II previously cut for horse and floor decoration. Trace three and follow manufacturer's instructions. Press the appliqué film on wrong side of two of the decorative pieces. Center these pieces and press in place as shown in illustration. Set the third piece aside, also with appliqué film pressed to wrong side of fabric, for later use. Place a piece of tear-away stabilizer behind the appliqués and satin stitch around edges with medium-wide stitch and coordinating thread.

13. For section I, use diagonal corner technique to make one of unit 55. Join units 56 and 57, then add unit 55 to left side of these units. Join unit 54 to top of combined units to complete section I.

14. For section J, use diagonal corner technique to make one of unit 59. Join units 59 and 60 as shown; then add unit 58 to top to complete section J.

15. For section K, use diagonal corner technique to make one of unit 64. To assemble section, begin by joining units 61 and 62, then add unit 63 to bottom of combined units. Join units 64 and 65 and join the resulting unit to combined units 61-63 to complete section K.

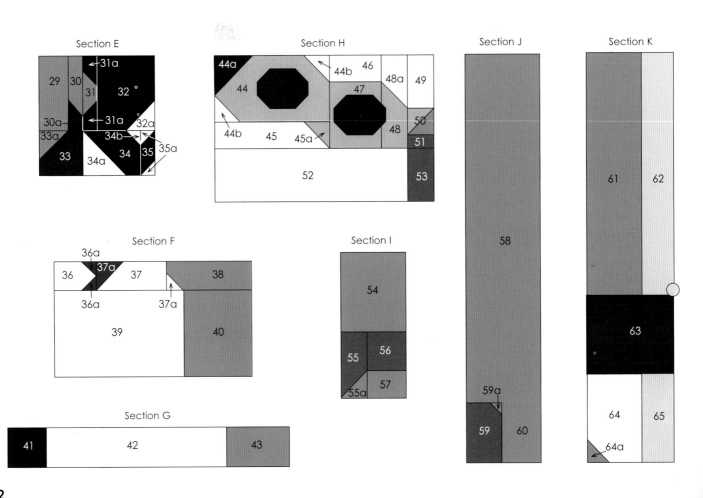

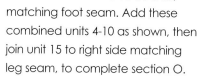

16. To construct section L, use diagonal end technique to make one each of units 69 and 70. Use diagonal corner technique to make one each of units 68, 71, 72, 73, and 76. For unit 69, refer to unit 69 construction illustration and make diagonal end first, then add diagonal corners in alphabetical order. Trim seam on diagonal corner 69b and press out, then add diagonal corner 69c.

17. Join units 69 and 70 as shown, matching diagonal seams. Join unit 68 to top of these combined units, then join unit 67 to left side. Join units 73 and 74, then add unit 72 to left side. Join unit 71 to top of these combined units and unit 75 to bottom. Join units 77 and 78, then add unit 76 to top, matching seams. Join combined units 71-75 to combined units 76-78, matching seams. Pin and stitch the two combined unit sections together, matching all diagonal seams to complete section L.

18. For section M, use diagonal corner technique to make one each of units 81, 83, 84, 85, 88, and 89. Use diagonal end technique to make one of unit 82.

19. For section M assembly, begin by joining units 79 and 80; then add unit 81 to right side of combined units. Join units 82 and 83 as shown, then add unit 84 to right side. Join the two sections together as shown, matching diagonal seam. Join units 86 and 87. Add unit 85 to top of combined 86-87 units and unit 88 to bottom, matching seams. Join units 90 and 91, then add unit 89 to left side, matching seams. Join combined units 85-88 to left side. Join this section to top portion to complete section M.

20. Referring to illustration of horse top on page 61, join sections B and C together as shown. Take care to match seams on units 7 and 18. Add section D directly below combined sections B-C, making sure to match mane and neck as shown in illustration. Join sections E and F, then add these combined sections to horse head section, again matching mane. Join section G directly below

these combined sections, matching saddle and chest seams. Join sections H and I, matching leg seams, and add these combined sections to assembled horse head. Add section J to right side of horse front and section K to left side of horse front, matching leg seam on section J and saddle seams on section K.

21. Join sections L and M, taking care to match horse back seam, breeching, and tail seams. Add unit 66 to top of combined sections L-M, then join the resulting unit to horse front, matching saddle and horse body seams.

22. Cut a 21" piece of gold braid. To insert reins, rip open small section in seam, indicated by a circle between units 21 and 18. Insert gold braided trim about ³⁄₈" between units and pin in place. Stitch seam back together, securing this section several times so that trim does not loosen. Open a small section of seam, indicated by second circle, between units 62 and 33. Insert remaining end of braided trim as before being sure to let braid drape softly as shown in photograph. Close seam, securing several times.

23. Join section A to top of horse top section, matching pole seams to complete horse top.

24. Use a gold metallic satin stitch on saddle, stitching ¼" from all edges.

Horse Bottom

1. To make horse bottom, begin by joining units 1, 2, and 3 in a row as shown to complete section N.

2. To assemble section O, use diagonal corner technique to make one each of units 4, 6, 10, 12, and 15. Join units 5 and 6 together. Join units 7 and 8 together, then add unit 9 to bottom of combine units 7-8. Add combined units 5-6 to left side, then add unit 4 across top and unit 10 to bottom of these combined units. Join units 11 and 12. Join units 13 and 14 as shown. Join the 11-12 units to the 13-14 units, matching foot seam. Add these combined units 4-10 as shown, then join unit 15 to right side matching leg seam, to complete section O.

3. For section P, begin by using diagonal corner technique to make one each of units 16 and 20. Use diagonal end technique to make one of unit 19. Join units 17 and 18, then add unit 16 to top of these combined units. Join units 19 and 20,

Unit 69

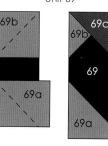

Section L

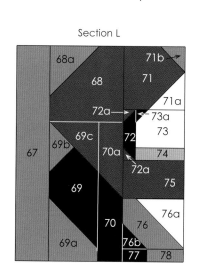

Section M

then add them to left side of combined units 16-18 as shown to complete section P.

4. For section Q, use diagonal corner technique to make one each of units 22, 24, 25, 29, 30, 34, 35, and 37. Use

diagonal end technique to make one of unit 21. After pressing out diagonal end, add diagonal corner 21b.

5. To assemble section Q, begin by joining units 23 and 24; then add unit 22 to top of these combined units, matching leg seam. Join unit 25 to right side, then add unit 21 to top of these combined units matching diagonal leg seam. Join units 26, 27, and 28 in a row. Join units 29, 30, and 31 as shown. Stitch these two rows together, then add them to bottom of combined units 21-25. Join units 32 and 33 and add them to left side of completed back feet. Join units 35 and 36, then add unit 37 to bottom of these combined units as shown. Join unit 34 to left side, then add unit 38 to bottom. Join unit 39 to left side. Join the two combined unit sections together to complete section Q.

Section Q

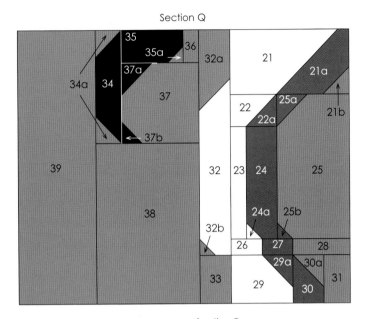

Section N

Section P

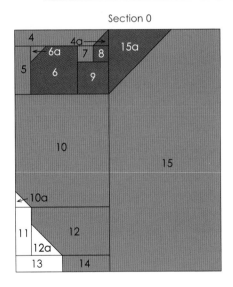

Section 0

Horse Bottom

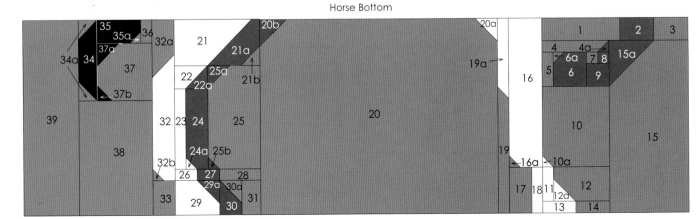

My Carousel

6. To assemble horse bottom, refer to horse bottom illustration on page 64 and begin by joining section N to top of section O as shown, matching leg seams. Join sections P and Q together, matching diagonal leg seam. Join the front leg and back leg sections together to complete horse bottom.

Quilt Top Assembly

1. To make outer poles, join two $3\frac{1}{2}$" x 29" strips end to end. Make two and press seams. The completed poles should measure $3\frac{1}{2}$" x $57\frac{1}{2}$". Refer to photograph of quilt; note that lace on poles are placed at a 45° angle. Beginning with right pole, notice the direction of the lines. First line should begin on bottom left corner of pole. Draw lines to pole top. You should have eighteen lines.

2. Cut appliqué film into $\frac{1}{2}$" strips and press them to the back of the white lace. We use a product called Steam-A-Seam2®. This product fuses the lace (or fabric) to the background and in our experience with this product we have found that it holds permanently, alleviating the necessity of topstitching the lace in place. Refer to manufacturer's instructions for use of any appliqué film.

3. Lay lace along diagonal lines and cut to fit. Cut the lace with scissors or rotary cutter at edges so that it will be sewn into the seams. Press in place. Repeat this procedure for remaining pole with lines mirror-imaged as shown.

4. To make long side borders from fabric 1, join two 5" x 29" strips end to end. Make two and press seams. The completed borders should measure 5" x $57\frac{1}{2}$". Refer to photograph of quilt and join the borders to outside edges of poles as shown, catching lace in seams. Press seams.

5. Join poles to completed horse sides as shown, making sure that lace in sewn into the seams.

6. Referring to the illustration, draw the quilting design onto 5" x 12" pillar base previously cut as directed from fabric II. You may either quilt or satin stitch the design with gold metallic thread. Following manufacturer's instructions for appliqué film, trace the pillar base onto appliqué film. Press appliqué film to back of pillar base. Center pillar base top over pole so that pillar base bottom lines up with raw edge of side and bottom. Press in place. If you have chosen to satin stitch the design onto the pillar base, place tear-away stabilizer behind it and stitch design now. Satin stitch around edges of pillar base that will not be sewn into seams. Tear away the stabilizer.

Pillar Base

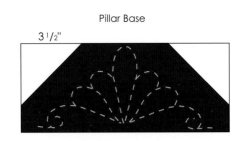

3$\frac{1}{2}$"

7. For decorative floor, join the two $4\frac{1}{4}$" x $30\frac{1}{2}$" strips from fabric V. Press seams. The completed floor should measure $4\frac{1}{4}$" x $60\frac{1}{2}$". As for decorations on horse, draw twelve decorative shapes (using decorative piece cut from fabric II) onto appliqué film. Press onto wrong side of decorative pieces. Referring to photograph of quilt, begin placing decorative pieces as shown. First decorative piece should be centered in $4\frac{1}{4}$" width, 1" from each outer short edge. Remaining decorative pieces are spaced approx. 2" apart and centered widthwise as shown. When you are satisfied with placement, press decorative pieces in place. Using tear-away stabilizer behind the floor, satin stitch decorative pieces in place. Tear stabilizer away when you are done with the satin stitching. Join the floor to bottom of horse section, sewing pillar bases into seams.

8. Join horse section to canopy section making certain that scallops on canopy are wrong side up as in canopy illustration with right sides of scallops to right side of canopy top. Place top edge of horse section along bottom raw edge of canopy top, right sides together. Using an accurate $\frac{1}{4}$" seam, stitch horse section to canopy, catching scallops in your stitching. Press scallops down.

9. For outer scalloped edges, refer to photograph of quilt and join scallops together for sides as shown. Make certain that colors are placed correctly. Join fourteen together for each side, alternating colors. Join the scallops to each side.

10. Join bottom scallops together as shown in illustration, adding triangles to each end. Join this scallop section across bottom of quilt, matching triangles to side scallops. Trim triangles if necessary. Cut $2\frac{1}{2}$"-wide bias binding from fabric II, making 445" of continuous bias binding. Bind quilt.

11. Complete details by sewing a $\frac{7}{8}$" button at beginning of reins as shown. Sew $\frac{1}{2}$" buttons in center of all decorative pieces of fabric II on horse. Additional buttons may be sewn on outer scallops of fabric II if desired.

12. This quilt fits top of a double bed with scallops hanging down over three sides. Canopy fits over top of pillows with a small pillow tuck and canopy scallops laying flat at bottom of pillows.

On the Road

FABRIC TIPS This quilt is wonderful for a child who loves to run little cars all over his or her bed, so we wanted bright, primary jewel tones to make an inviting village for a small person. Lime and navy are a dynamite combination to generate just the right contrast between the village green, the pockets, and the highlights in the village buildings. We chose a lime print that suggests grass with tiny vines and leaves. Our navy fabric is a texture print with dark navy lines over a lighter background, and the red and green are the same texture print. The gray we used for the road is a print that resembles small gravel. Dramatic effects are the key, rather than an overall repetitive tonal quality.

Materials

▨ Fabric I	(gray texture print)	2¼ yards
☐ Fabric II	(solid white)	1½ yard
▨ Fabric III	(lime print)	4 yards
■ Fabric IV	(navy texture print)	1⅞ yards
▨ Fabric V	(bright yellow stripe)	¼ yard
▨ Fabric VI	(solid bright orange)	⅛ yard
▨ Fabric VII	(medium brown batik)	⅛ yard
▨ Fabric VIII	(red texture print)	¼ yard
▨ Fabric IX	(dark-green textured print)	½ yard
■ Fabric X	(black print)	¼ yard
▨ Fabric XI	(solid light blue)	⅜ yard
Backing		5 yards
Batting		70" x 92"
Appliqué film		¾ yard
Tear-away stabilizer		¾ yard
Velcro® Dots for signs		
Template plastic for signs		

Cutting

▨ *From Fabric I, cut: (gray texture print)*

• Two 14"-wide strips. From these, cut:
  Four - 14" squares (C1a)
  Two - 2½" x 4" (F28)
  One - 2¼" x 7" (E3)
  Eight - 1¾" x 3½" (2, 6)
  Six - 1¾" x 2¼" (6d)
  Six - 1¾" squares (6a)
  One - 1½" x 3½" (D15)
• Twenty-eight 1¾"-wide strips for strip set 1.

On the Road

64" x 86"
Finished size for top of bed: 38" x 73" with a 13" drop.
Designed by Pam Bono and Mindy Kettner.
Quilted by Faye Gooden.

☐ *From Fabric II, cut: (solid white)*

• One 14½"-wide strip. From this, cut:
  Two - 14½" squares (C1)
  One - 6" x 6½" (E2)
  One - 1" x 6¼" (E19)
  One - 3⅜" square (One Way sign)
  One - 3½" square (Do Not Enter sign)
  Two - 1½" x 4" (E10a)
  Two - 1¼"x 4½" (E14)
  One - 2¼"x 5" (E15)

• One 3½"-wide strip. From this, cut:
  One - 2¾" x 3½" (Speed Limit sign)
  Four - 1" x 3½" (2a, 3a)
  Four - 2" x 2½" (D10)
  Three - 1½" x 2½" (E8, E17, E18)
  One - 1¼" x 2½" (E19)
  Six - 1" x 2¼" (6c)
  Six - 1" x 1¾" (6b)
  Four - 1½" squares (E13a, E16a)
  Four - ¾" x ¾" (baseball bases)
• Fourteen - 1"-wide strips for strip set 1.
• Use scraps for street signs.

▨ *From Fabric III, cut: (lime print)*

• One 14½"-wide strip. From this, cut:
  Two - 8" x 14½" (F31)
  One - 3¼" x 14½" (D22)
  Two - 2½" x 14½" (A9, B11)
  One - 1½" x 14½" (E20)
  One - 1" x 14½" (E5)
  One - 12½" square (C1b)
  One - 1½" x 11¾" (D1)

• One 12½"-wide strip. From this, cut:
  Three - 12½" squares (C1b)
  One - 4½" x 12½" (B10)

• Five 9½"-wide strips. From these, cut:
  One - 9½" x 38½"(10)
  Four - 9½" x 36½" (12) Piece to equal two 72½" long strips.
  Two - 1½" x 9½" (16)
  Two - 1½" x 8½" (15)
  One - 3¼" x 7½" (E6)
  One - 2½" x 7¼" (F27)
  One - 4¼" x 7" (E4)
  Two - 2½" x 6½" (A8)
  Two - 2¼" squares (D7a)
  One - 2" x 6" (E1)
  One - 2" x 2½" (F29)
  Four - 1½" squares (D3a, E7a)
  One - 1¼" x 2½" (F30)
  One - 1¼" x 1½" (D5)
• One 6½" wide strip. From this, cut:
  Two - 5½" x 6½" (A1)
  One - 6½" x 11¾" (D21)

Cut remainder into one 3½" strip and one 3" strip. From these, cut:

    One - 3½" x 12½" (B9)
    Two - 3" x 4" (E10a)
    Two - 3" x 3¼" (D2)
    Two - 2½" x 3" (E9)
    Two - 2½" squares (A2a)

• Nine 2½"-wide strips (eight for straight-grain binding). From remaining strip, cut:

    Six - 2½" squares (A10a, F2a, 14a)
    One - 2¼" x 16½" (F1)

• Eight 1½"-wide strips pieced together for outer borders 20 and 21.

From Fabric IV, cut: (navy texture print)

• Two 8½"-wide strips. From these, cut:

    Two - 8½" squares (14) Cut one from each strip.
    Two - 7½" x 33½" (15). Piece to equal
    one 66½" long pocket.

• Eight 5½"-wide strips. From these, cut:

    Two - 7½" x 36½" (11)
    Six - 7½" x 33½" (15). Piece to equal three 66½"
    long pockets.
    One - 2½" x 4½" (F5)
    Three - 1½" x 4½" (A13)
    Three - 1½" x 2½" (A12, A14)

From Fabric V, cut: (bright yellow stripe)

• One 5"-wide strip. From this, cut:

    One - 4" x 5" (F20)
    Two - 3⅝" x 4½" (Yield signs)
    Three - 1½" x 4½" (A5)
    One - 4" x 4¼" (F14)
    One - 2½" x 3½" (F8)
    Five - 2½" squares (A11, B5)
    Two - 2" x 2½" (F17)
    Three - 1½" x 2½" (A4, A6)
    Two - 1¾" x 2" (F24)
    Four - ¾" x 1¼" (F16, F21)

From Fabric VI, cut: (solid bright orange)

• One 3½"-wide strip. From this, cut:

    Two - 3½" x 4½" (cones)
    One - 2½" x 4½" (F12)

From Fabric VII, cut: (medium brown batik)

• One 2"-wide strip. From this, cut:

    One - 2" x 5¾" (bleachers for stadium)
    One - 2" x 3½" (E13)
    Two - 1" x 3" (E12)
    One - ⅝" x 1¼" (pitcher's mound)

From Fabric VIII, cut: (red textured print)

• One 3½"-wide strip. From this, cut:

    Four - 3½" squares (Stop sign & School sign)
    Two - 2½" x 3½" (A7, A15)
    One - 1" x 3½" (D14)
    One - 2½" x 7½" (A10)
    One - 2" x 2½" (D9)
    One - 1½" x 2½" (D6)
    Three - 1" x 2½" (D12)
    Two - ¾" x 2½" (F15, F22)
    One - 1½" x 5" (D19)
    One - 1" x 5" (D13)
    One - 1" x 2" (D11)

• One 1½"-wide strip. From this, cut:

    Two - 1½" squares (D15a)
    One - 1¼" x 7½" (D8)
    Two - 1" x 1¼" (D4)
    One - 1" x 6½" (D20)

From Fabric IX, cut: (dark-green textured print)

• One 7½"-wide strip. From this, cut:

    One - 4" x 7½" (E10)
    One - 2½" x 7½" (A2)
    One - 2" x 7¼" (F7)
    One - 3⅜" square (baseball field)
    One - 2½" x 3" (E11)

• Cut remainder into three 2½"-wide strips. From these, cut:

    One - 2½" x 9¾" (F26)
    One - 2½" x 4" (F10)
    One - 2½" square (D17)
    One - 1½" x 2½" (E7)
    One - 1" x 2½" (F9)
    One - 2" x 6½" (F19)
    One - 2" x 3" (F3)
    One - 1¾" x 3" (F6)
    One - 1¼" x 6½" (F25)
    One - 1¼" x 4½" (F13)
    Two - 1" x 4½" (F4, F11)

• Four 1"-wide strips. From these, cut:

    Two - 1" x 37½" (border 7)
    Two - 1" x 36½" (border 9). Piece to equal 72½" long.

From Fabric X, cut: (black print)

• One 3½"-wide strip. From this, cut:

    One - 3½" x 4½" (B1)
    Two - 2½" x 4½" (traffic lights)
    One - 1½" x 3½" (D16)
    One - 2½" x 16½" (F2)
    One - 2½" square (A3)
    One - 1½" x 2½" (D3)
    Three - 1" x 2½" (D18, F18)
    One - 1" x 1¾" (F23)

• One 2¼"-wide strip. From this, cut:
    One - 2¼" x 7½" (D7)
    One - 1¾" x 7½" (B8)

    From Fabric XI, cut: (solid light blue)

• One 2½"-wide strip. From this, cut:
    Three - 2½" x 4½" (B2, E16)
    Two - 1½" x 7¼" (B7)
    Two - 1½" x 2½" (B6)
    Two - 1½" x 5½" (B4)

• One 1¼"-wide strip. From this, cut:
    One - 1¼" x 5 ½" (B3)

• Two 1"-wide strips. From these, cut:
    Two - 1" x 36½" (border 8). Piece to equal 72½" long.

Assembly

House Block A

Block A

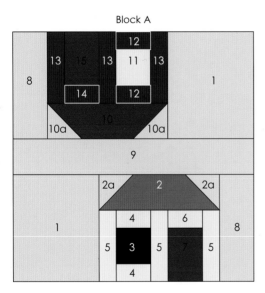

1. To assemble block A, use diagonal corner technique on page 8 to make one each of units 2 and 10. Join units 4, 3, and 4 in a row as shown; then add unit 5 to opposite sides. Repeat this procedure for units 12, 11, and 12, adding unit 13 to opposite sides of resulting combined unit.

2. Join units 6 and 7, then add unit 5 to right side as illustrated. Join units 14 and 15, then add 13 to the right side.

3. Join the window and door sections of the houses together, then join roof units 2 and 10. Join unit 1 to left side of each house, and unit 8 to right side. Complete the block by joining house sections to unit 9 as illustrated.

Office Building Block B

Block B

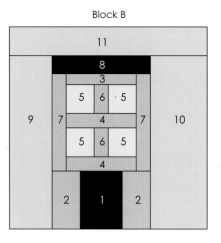

1. Referring to block B diagram, begin by joining units 5, 6, and 5 in a row as shown. Make two. Make a vertical row of units 3, 5-6-5, 4, 5-6-5, and 4, then add unit 7 to opposite sides of window section as shown. Join unit 8 to top of this completed building section.

2. Join units 2, 1, and 2 together in a horizontal row, then add it to the building bottom. Join unit 9 to left side and unit 10 to right side, then add unit 11 across top to complete block B.

Side Road Block C

Block C

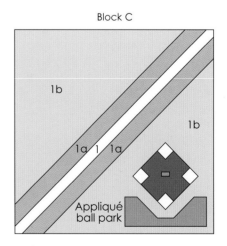

1. Use diagonal corner technique to make two of block C. Begin by adding diagonal corners 1a. Trim seam and press outwards. Join diagonal corners 1b and press out.

2. Add ball park stadium to one block C using the pattern provided for the bleachers (page 75). Trace onto appropriate fabric and cut out. Use our appliqué method described on page 11. Place tear-away stabilizer behind your ball park appliqué and satin stitch in place.

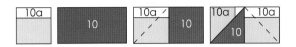

School Block D

Block D

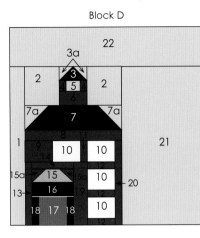

1. To make school block D, use diagonal corner technique to make one each of units 3, 7, and 15. Make the bell tower first by joining units 4, 5, and 4 in a row, then add unit 3 to row top, and add unit 6 to row bottom. Join background unit 2 to opposite sides of bell tower as illustrated in block D diagram.

2. Make a vertical row of windows by joining units 10, 12, 10, 12, 10, and 12 as shown. Join unit 20 to right side of this window row.

3. Join units 9, 10, and 11 in a horizontal row as shown and set aside. Join units 18, 17, and 18 in a row. Join units 14, 15, and 16, then add them to top of door section. Join unit 13 to left side and join unit 19 to right side.

4. Add combined units 9-11 to top of combined units 13-19 as illustrated. Join the combined vertical window section to right side of completed door section, then join unit 8 to top. Join roof unit 7 to top of school bottom, then add bell tower section as shown.

5. Join unit 1 to left side of school and unit 21 to right side, then join unit 22 to top to complete block D.

Church Block E

Block E

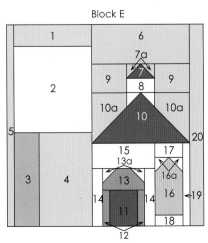

1. Refer to block E diagram and begin by using diagonal corner technique to make one each of units 7, 10, 13, and 16.

2. Refer to illustration for making unit 10. Join pieces 10a from fabrics II and III as shown to make the 10a diagonal corner. Place one diagonal corner on left side of unit 10 as shown and stitch diagonally from corner to corner. Trim seam and press outwards. Place remaining diagonal corner as shown and stitch. Trim seam and press out.

3. For parking lot, join units 1 and 2. Join units 3 and 4, then join these to bottom of combined units 1-2. Join unit 5 to left side to complete parking lot.

4. For steeple, join units 7 and 8, then add unit 9 to opposite sides of these combined units. Join unit 6 to top of combined units 7-9 and completed roof unit 10 to bottom.

5. For church, join units 12, 11, and 12 in a row, then add unit 13 to top. Join unit 14 to opposite sides of door section, then add unit 15 to top.

6. Join units 17, 16, and 18 in a vertical row as shown, then add unit 19 to right side of this combined unit.

7. Join door and window sections together, then add roof and steeple section. Join parking lot to left side of church and unit 20 to right side of church to complete block E.

Auto Repair Block F

Block F

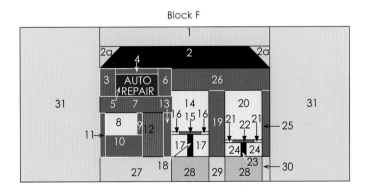

1. Use diagonal corner technique to make one of unit 2. To begin assembly, join units 1 and 2.

2. Auto Repair sign: refer to instructions on page 73 for making signs and use pattern on page 76. The completed sign will become unit 5, which will be pieced into the next step.

3. Join units 4 and 5. Join units 3, 4-5, and 6 in a horizontal row; then add unit 7 to bottom. Join units 8 and 9, then add unit 10 to bottom of these combined units. Join unit 11

to left side. Join units 12 and 13, then add them to right side of window section. Join window/door section to Auto Repair sign section.

4. For bay door section, begin by joining units 16, 15, and 16. Join units 21, 22, and 21. Join units 17, 18, and 17 in a row. Repeat with units 24, 23, and 24. Join the combined units 15-16 to combined units 17-18 as shown, then add unit 14 to top. Repeat with 21-22 and 23-24 units, joining unit 20 to top.

5. Join combined units 14-18 in a row with unit 19. Join combined units 20-24, and unit 25. Join these combined sections; then add unit 26 to top. Join the bay door section with auto repair section. Add combined units 1-2 to top.

6. Join units 27, 28, 29, 28, and 30 in a row and add to bottom of auto shop. Add unit 31 to opposite sides of shop as shown to complete block F.

Strip Set 1 For Roads and Intersections

1. Join two 1¾'' strips of fabric I with one 1'' strip of fabric II as shown in the diagram for strip set 1. Make fourteen strip sets. Press seams towards darkest fabric.

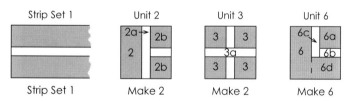

Strip Set 1	Unit 2	Unit 3	Unit 6
Strip Set 1	Make 2	Make 2	Make 6

2. For road unit 1, cut eleven 14½'' segments referring to quilt assembly diagram. For road unit 4, cut one 31½'' segment. For road unit 5, cut four 33'' segments and piece them together to equal two 65½'' pieces. For road unit 18, cut two 28½'' segments and piece together to equal one 56½'' piece. For road unit 19, cut four 41'' segments and piece them together to equal two 82½'' pieces. Mark each road piece with its unit number for reference. Leftover scraps may be used for smaller segment pieces.

3. For intersection unit 2, cut two 1¾'' segments. For intersection unit 3, cut four 1¾'' segments. For intersection unit 6, join 1¾'' squares of fabric I (unit 6a) to 1'' x 1¾'' pieces of fabric II (unit 6b). Add 1'' x 2¼'' piece of fabric II (unit 6c) to left side of combined 6a-6b units, then join 1¾'' x 2¼'' piece of fabric I (unit 6d) to bottom of combined units. Join unit 6 to left side. Referring to small block drawings, piece side intersections of each block together as shown.

Town Quilt Section

1. To assemble town, begin by joining house and office building blocks with a road 1 strip between them.

2. Referring to quilt assembly diagram, join school block and one side road block (with stadium appliqué) with road 1 strip between them.

3. Join remaining side road block and church block with a road 1 strip between them as shown.

4. Make two sets of road 1 strips with a #2 intersectionblock between them. Join one resulting row to top of office building/house section. Make two sets of road 1 strips separated by intersection #3 as illustrated. Join one of these sets to bottom of office building/ house section. Join one remaining road section between school and church sections, then add last road 1 section with a #2 intersection to bottom of church section.

5. Join office building/house section to assembled town center and auto repair shop to bottom. Join road 4 to bottom of town center.

6. Join intersection 6 corners to top and bottom of road 5 sections as shown, so road circles the town. Join these long road sections to opposite sides of town, matching road corner seams.

7. Join shoulder grass border 7 from fabric IX to top and bottom of town. Join pieced shoulder grass border 9 to right side of town, and pieced river border 8 to left side of town.

Overnight Parking Pockets and Borders

1. Make four sets of long pockets: two for the pockets and two for pocket linings. Join two 7½'' x 33½'' pieces of fabric IV to create one set which equals 66½''. Make the four sets. Place two sets right sides together and stitch around 3 sides, leaving one long side open. Trim corners, turn right side out, and press. Repeat for other side pocket. With a chalk marker, mark the pockets into eleven 3''-wide sections.

2. For bottom pocket, place the 7½'' x 36½'' pieces of fabric IV right sides together and stitch as for long side pockets. Mark six 3''-wide sections.

3. Position side pockets (unit 15) on unit 12 so that each pocket is centered and bottom raw edge is against one long raw edge of unit 12. Baste in place. Stitch pocket to unit 12 on each short side, and down each previously marked chalk line. Be sure to stay stitch at pocket tops as

they will get a lot of wear. Join completed side pocket (unit 12) to opposite sides of quilt top.

4. Center pocket 11 on unit 10 as for side pockets, matching raw edges along long bottom. Stitch short sides in place and down marked chalk lines.

5. Use diagonal corner technique to make two of unit 14, checking position of diagonal corners as they are mirror images. Refer to Block F diagram and join unit 15 to appropriate side, then add unit 16 as shown. Be certain to check diagram as the position of these two units are a bit different for each unit 14. Join unit 14 to opposite short sides of completed bottom pocket (unit 10) as shown. Join this section to bottom of quilt.

6. Join unit 18 road to bottom of quilt, catching pocket bottom into a $1/4$" seam. Join remaining intersection #6 blocks to bottom of road 19 pieces, positioning them as shown in drawing. Join the resulting set to sides of quilt.

Finishing

1. Join border 20 to top and bottom of quilt and border 21 to sides.

2. Quilt as desired, being sure to quilt down pocket lines so that pockets are secured through all thicknesses.

3. Make 315" of straight-grain binding from fabric III and french-fold bind the quilt.

Signs

1. Sew large Velcro® dots to places on quilt where you wish to attach signs.

2. We suggest using fabric pens to make street signs with the names of streets in your neighborhood. For colored signs such as the traffic lights and stop signs, we have given you the signs reversed so that you might take them to a T-shirt shop that makes heat transfers. The signs may be printed (using a computer printer) or photocopied onto photo transfer paper and heat transferred onto white fabric. For the cones, we used orange fabric.

3. We used one sheet of template plastic. Rather than cutting the plastic the size marked by the dotted lines on the patterns, we cut it the size marked by the solid lines. Pull the printed signs around the template plastic and glue the $1/4$" allowance around on the back. You may also want to use Fray check® to keep edges from raveling. We attached the other side of the Velcro dots to the back and found that when we used a leather needle in our sewing machines, we were able to secure the edges of the signs and also sew the Velcro dots down securely. Place the signs on the quilt.

Quilt Assembly

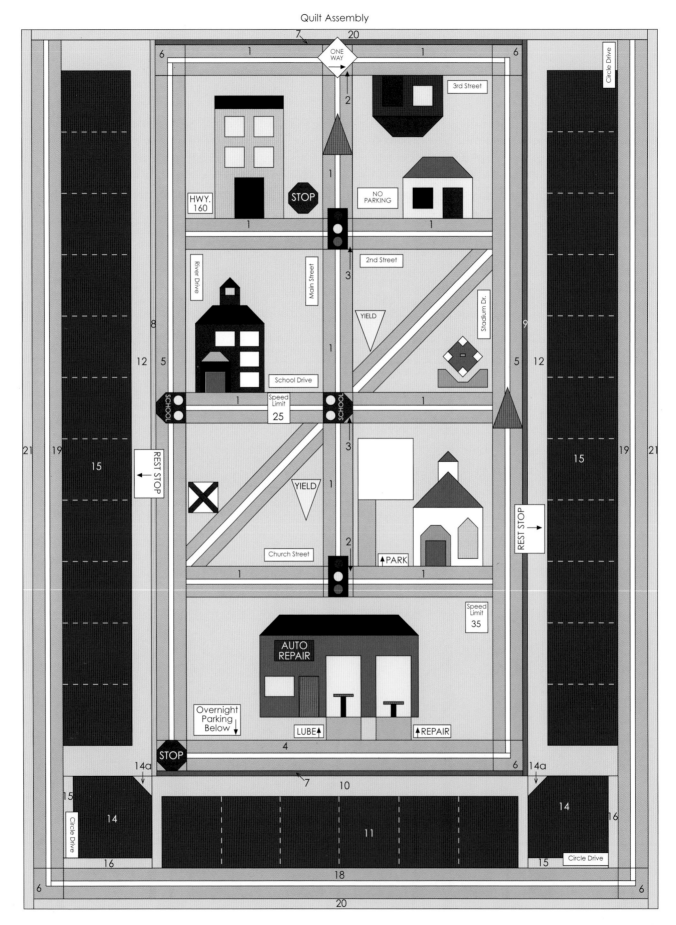

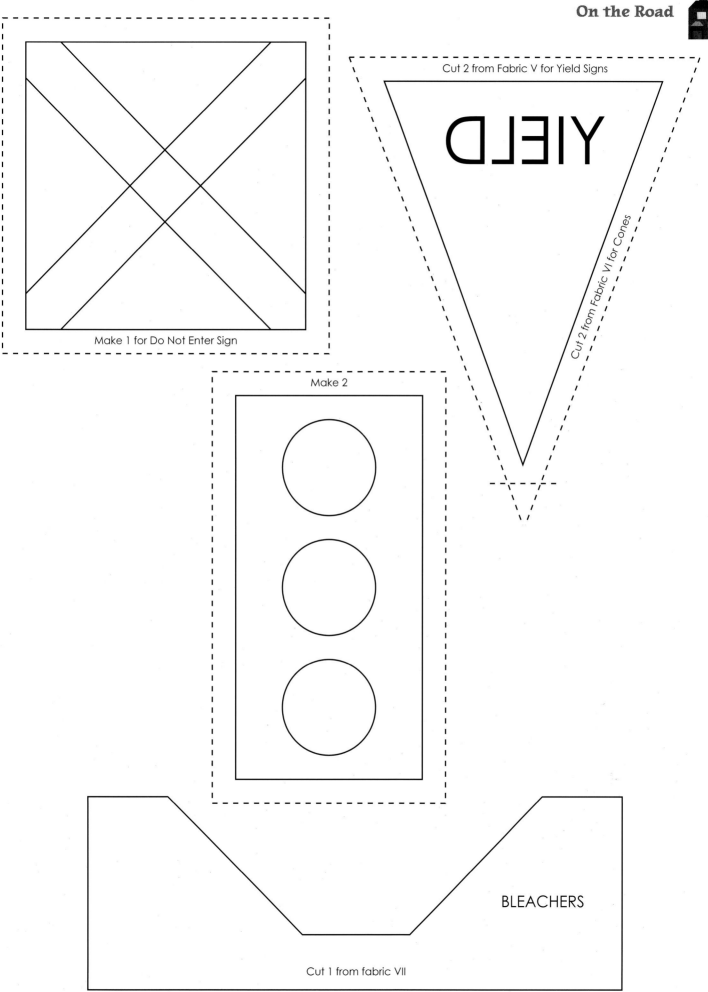

Make 1 for Do Not Enter Sign

Cut 2 from Fabric V for Yield Signs

YIELD

Cut 2 from Fabric VI for Cones

Make 2

BLEACHERS

Cut 1 from fabric VII

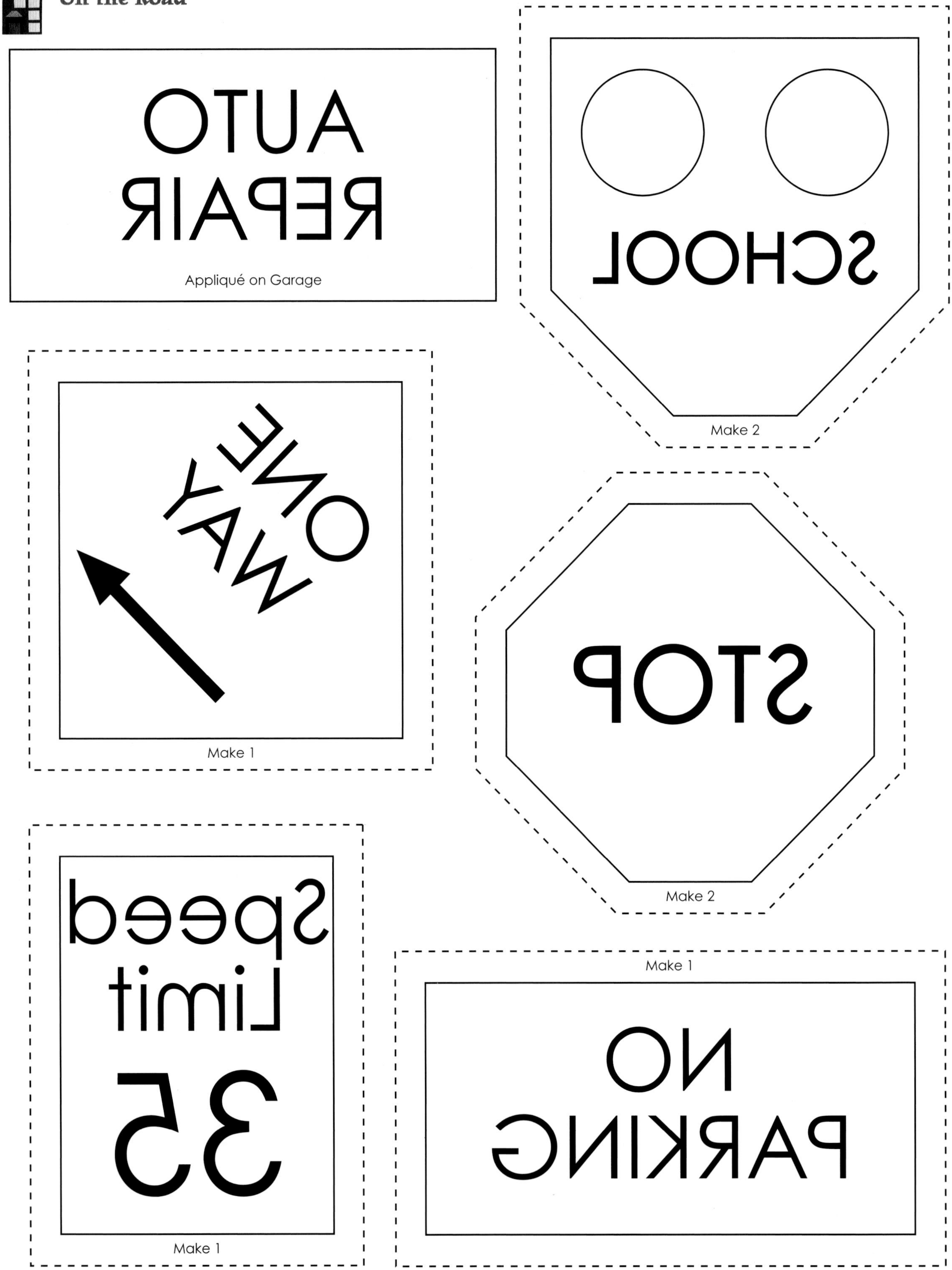

AUTO REPAIR

Appliqué on Garage

SCHOOL

Make 2

ONE WAY

Make 1

STOP

Make 2

Speed Limit 35

Make 1

NO PARKING

Make 1

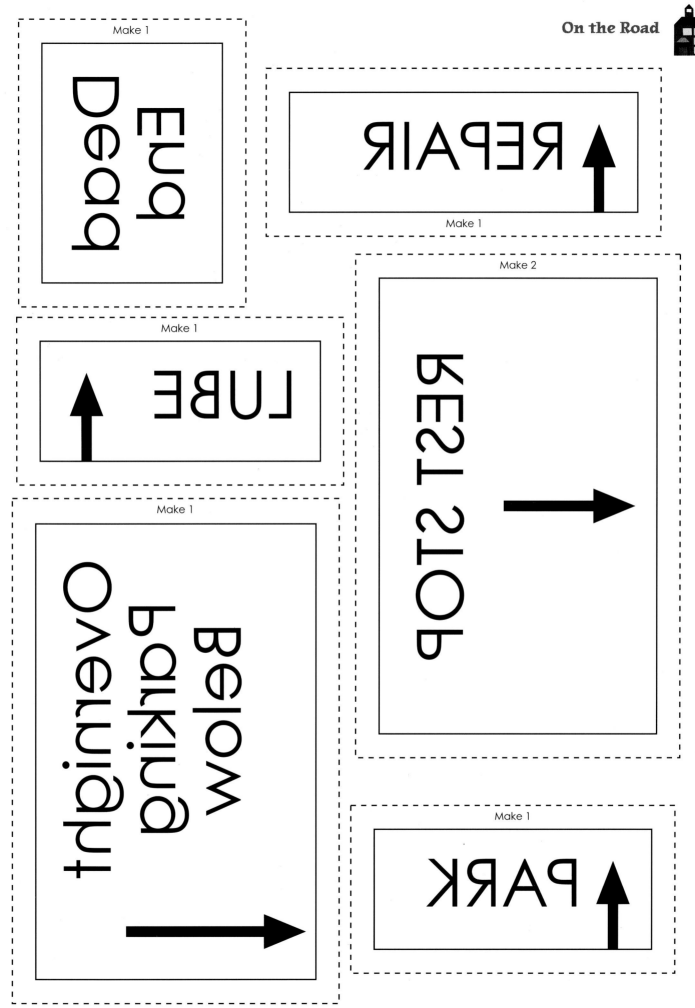

Make 1

Dead End

Make 1

REPAIR ↑

Make 1

LUBE ↑

Make 2

REST STOP →

Make 1

Overnight
parking
below →

Make 1

PARK ↑

✖ Race Day

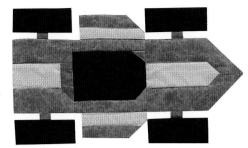

FABRIC TIPS We used a bright green print for our infield to give the appearance of well-manicured grass. We tried several fabrics for the track, including a dark brown for a dirt track, and found that the cars showed up best on the gray pebble fabric. Choose bright colors for each car, so they contrast with the background.

Materials

▢	Fabric I	(gray pebble print)	3¾ yards
▨	Fabric II	(bright green print)	3¾ yards
▨	Fabric III	(light gray solid)	¼ yard
▨	Fabric IV	(medium gray solid)	⅛ yard
■	Fabric V	(solid black)	1⅝ yards
▢	Fabric VI	(solid white)	¼ yard
▨	Fabric VII	(dark gold print)	⅜ yard

** Add an additional ⅛ yard if used for cars.

▨	Fabric VIII	(light gold solid)	Scrap
▨	Fabric IX	(dark brown check)	Scrap
	Fabric X	(varied colors for car bodies)	⅛ yard
	Appliqué film		¼ yard
	Tear-away pellon		¼ yard
	Backing		6 yards
	Batting		84" x 106"

Race Day

78" x 99¾"
Infield finished size: 50¼" x 72"
Designed by Dallas,
Robert, and Pam Bono.
Quilted by Faye Gooden.

Cutting

▢ *From Fabric I, cut: (gray pebble print)*

- Three 15½"-wide strips. From these, cut:
  Four - 15½" squares (1b)
  Two - 5" x 15½" (2)
  Two - 4¼" x 15½" (6)
  One - 3⅞" x 15½" (B3)
  Fourteen - 2⅜" x 15½" (A17)
  Two - 2" x 15½" (3)

- From scrap, cut:
  Two - 2¾" squares (B9)
  Four - 2" squares (B4a, B11)

- Six 12½"-wide strips. From these, cut:
  Two - 12½" x 34⅞" (11)
  Two - 12½" x 27⅛" (8)
  Two - 12½" x 23⅜" (10)
  Two - 9½" x 12½" (9)
  Two - 6⅞" x 12½" (7)

- From scrap, cut:
  Two - 3½" x 7¼" (B2)
  Two - 5¾" x 6⅞" (B5)
  Four - 4¼" squares (1c)
  Fourteen - 2¾" x 4⅝" (A1)
  Fourteen - ⅞" x 5" (A12)

- Two 2" wide strips. From these, cut:
  Seventy - ⅞" x 2" (A5, A11)
  Fourteen - 1⅝" squares (A10a)

▨ *From Fabric II, cut: (bright green print)*

- Four 17"-wide strips. From these, cut:
  Four - 17" x 24½" (1)
  Two - 5¾" x 17¾" (5)
  Two - 3½" x 17¾" (4)

• From scrap, cut:
    Two - 9⅞" x 11¾" (C2)
    Four - 6⅞" squares (10a, 11a)
    Four - 4⅝" squares (D1a)
    Two - 3⅛" x 11" (C5)
    Two - 2⅜" x 14" (D7)
    Two - 2⅜" x 3⅛" (C7)
    Eight - 1¼" squares (C6a)

• One 3⅛"-wide strip. From this, cut:
    Two - 3⅛" x 18⅞" (C4)

• Two 2¾"-wide strips. From these, cut:
    Two - 2¾" x 21½" (C8)

• Nine 2½"-wide strips for straight-grain binding

• Nine 2⅜"-wide strips. From these, cut:
    Four - 2⅜" x 37⅝" (piece together to = 74¾"
    for Border 1)
    Five - 2⅜" x 42"(piece together end to end for
    Border 2)

■ *From Fabric III, cut: (light gray solid)*

• One 2¾"-wide strip. From this, cut:
    Six - 2¾" squares (D1b, D5)
    Two - 2" x 2¾" (D2)
    Two - 1¼" x 2" (D3)
    Fourteen - 1¼" squares (A17a)

• Two 1¼" wide strips. From these, cut:
    Seven - 1¼" x 8¾" (A16)

■ *From Fabric IV, cut: (medium gray solid)*

• One 2¾"-wide strip. From this, cut:
    One - 2¾" square (D6)
    Nine - 1¼" x 2" (A13, D3a)
    Fourteen - 1¼" squares (A15a)
    Twenty-eight - ⅞" x 1¼" (A4)

■ *From Fabric V, cut: (solid black)*

• Two 17"-wide strips. From these, cut:
    Four - 17" squares (1a)
    Four - 6⅛" squares (D1)
    Four - 2¾" x 3⅞" (D4)

• Two 3½"-wide strips. From these, cut:
    Seven - 3½" x 5" (A7)
    Two - 2" x 4¼" (A6)

• Two 2¾"-wide strips for strip set 1(Block C)

• Four 2" wide strips. From these, cut:
    Two - 2" x 24½" (12)
    Twenty-six - 2" x 4¼" (A6)

□ *From Fabric VI, cut: (solid white)*

• Two 2¾"-wide strips for strip set 1(Block C)

■ *From Fabric VII, cut: (dark gold print)*

• One 5⅜"-wide strip. From this, cut:
    One - 5⅜" x 13¼" (for trophy car appliqué)
    One - 5" x 6⅞" (B4)
    Two - 3½" squares (B5a)
    One - 2" x 3½" (B1)
    Two - 3⅛" squares (C6)

• One 1⅝"-wide strip. From this, cut:
    Two - 1⅝" x 18⅞" (C3)

• One 1¼"-wide strip. From this, cut:
    One - 1¼" x 11" (B8)
    Two - 1¼" x 2" (B7)

■ *From Fabric VIII, cut: (light gold solid)*

    One - 2" x 9½" (B6)

■ *From Fabric IX, cut: (dark brown check)*

    One - 2" x 12½" (B10)

From Fabric X, cut: (varied colors for cars and car accents.) For one car body, cut:

    Four - 2" x 4¼" (A3, A15)
    Two - 2¾" squares (A1a)
    Two - 1¼" x 5" (A8)
    Two - 1¼" x 4⅝" (A10)

For one car trim, cut:
    One - 2" x 4¼" (A2)
    One - 2" x 3½" (A14)
    Two - 1¼" x 4⅝" (A9)
    Four - 1¼" squares (A1b, A7a)

See photograph for color suggestions for each car.

Assembly

Block A

There are seven cars, each one made with different fabrics for the car bodies and trim.

1. Use diagonal corner technique on page 8 to make two mirror-image units each for units 1, combined units 9-10, 15, and 17. Use diagonal corner technique to make one of unit 7. For unit 1, add diagonal corners in alphabetical order as shown. For combined units 9-10, join units 9 and 10 as shown, then add diagonal corner 10a.

2. To assemble car, begin by joining units 3, 2, and 3 as illustrated in drawing of block A. Make four rows of units 5, 4, and 5. Add two of these combined units to opposite sides of combined units 3, 2, and 3, then join unit 6 wheels to opposite sides, making a horizontal row.

Block A

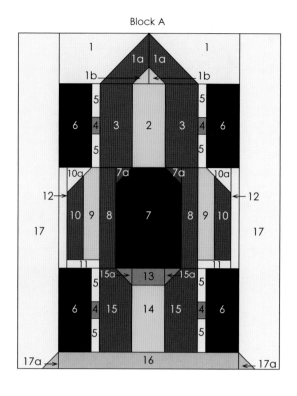

Block A

3. Join mirror-image units 1 as shown and join the resulting sets to car front units, matching seams.

4. For center car section, join units 8, 7, and 8 as shown. Join unit 11 to bottom of combined mirror-image units 9-10, then add unit 12 to sides. Refer to block A illustration for correct placement. Join mirror-image combined units 9-12 to opposite sides of center section. Join center section to front section, matching seams.

5. For rear section, begin by joining units 13 and 14; then add mirror-image units 15 to opposite sides. Join the remaining two 5, 4, and 5 units to opposite sides of combined units 13-15, then add unit 6 to opposite sides of the resulting row. Join unit 16 to bottom of rear section, then join rear section to car, matching seams.

6. Join mirror-image units 17 to opposite sides of car to complete Block A. Make seven of block A.

Block B

1. To assemble trophy block B, use diagonal corner technique to make one of unit 4 and two of mirror-image unit 5.

2. Join units 2, 1, and 2 in a horizontal row as shown, then add unit 3 to top of these combined units. Join units 5, 4, and 5 in a row as shown in the diagram of block B and add these to combined units 1-3, matching seams.

3. Join unit 7 to opposite short ends of unit 6, then add unit 8 to bottom of this horizontal row. Join unit 9 to opposite short ends, then join row to trophy bottom. Join units 11, 10, and 11 in a horizontal row, then add them to bottom of trophy.

4. Trace appliqué car (page 85) on wrong side of appliqué film and press onto dark gold fabric. Cut out and press onto trophy top. Satin stitch around car with coordinating thread. Draw or satin stitch in black around wheels. Using a black fabric pen, print the name of your favorite "racer" in unit 6 to complete block B. Make one.

Block C

1. Use 2¾"-wide strips of fabrics V and VI. Referring to strip set 1 illustration, join strips together as shown. Cut into ten 2¾" segments.

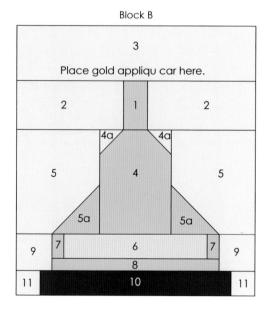

Block B

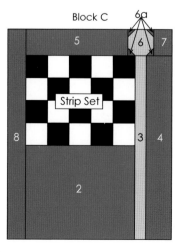

Block C

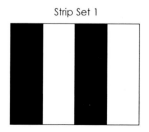

Strip Set 1

2. Join segments as shown in diagram of block C to make two flags (one facing left, one facing right).

3. Use diagonal corner technique to make one of unit 6. To assemble flag blocks, begin by joining assembled strip set 1 flag with unit 2 as shown. *Flag blocks are mirror images, so refer to block C illustration often for correct placement of units.*

4. Join units 3 and 4, then join them to flag, checking correct mirror image positioning for each of the two blocks.

5. Join units 5, 6, and 7 in a horizontal row, then add resulting row to top of flag, matching flag pole seam. Join unit 8 to side of flag (mirror imaged) to complete block C. Make two.

Block D

Block D

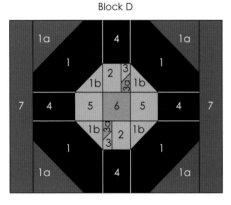

1. Use diagonal corner technique to make four mirror-image units 1. Use diagonal end technique to make two of unit 3.

2. To assemble block, begin at top of tire and join units 2 and 3; then add unit 4 to top of these combined units. Join mirror-image units 1 to opposite sides of combined units 2-4 as shown. Repeat this procedure for tire bottom row.

3. For center row, join units 4, 5, 6, 5, and 4 in a horizontal row as shown. Join tire top and bottom to this row as shown, matching seams, then add unit 7 to opposite sides of tire to complete block D. Make one. Using white fabric paint (we used correction fluid as it adheres well to the black fabric and washes well), print GOODWEAR on tire. You could also trace GOODWEAR onto the tire with white carbon paper and satin stitch.

Quilt Top Asembly

1. Referring to assembly diagram, begin by using diagonal corner technique to make four mirror image units 1. Add diagonal corners alphabetically, joining corner 1a first. Be sure to draw your diagonal clearly on this corner. After

adding to unit 1, trim seam and press out, then add diagonal corner 1b. Diagonal corner 1c is added last. Refer to quilt top diagram for the mirror image units. Two will be made slanting to the right, two slanting to the left.

2. Use diagonal corner technique to make two mirror image units 10 and 11 as shown.

3. To assemble quilt top, begin by adding unit 4 to top of one flag block C and one to bottom of mirror-image flag block C.

4. Join unit 5 to opposite sides of tire block D as shown, then join the flag blocks to each end, positioning them as shown in diagram.

5. For pit side of quilt top, join unit 3 to opposite sides of one car block A, then add unit 2 to top and bottom. Join mirror-image units 1 to top and bottom of car section as shown, then join this completed pit section to center section.

6. For trophy side of quilt top, join unit 6 to top and bottom of trophy block B, then join mirror image units 1 to top and bottom of trophy section as shown. Join resulting set to right side of center section to complete the infield.

7. Referring to illustration, make two car rows by joining unit 7, one car block A, unit 8, another car block A, and unit 9 in a vertical row. Make two rows. Refer to diagram frequently as cars must all be going in the same direction within each row. Join the car rows to opposite sides of quilt top as shown.

8. For top and bottom car rows, join unit 10, one car block A, and unit 11 in a row. Make two rows. Refer to illustration for proper placement and join the rows to top and bottom of quilt.

9. For border 1, join the two 2⅜" x 37⅝" strips of fabric II end to end. Make two. Join to top and bottom of quilt top.

10. For border 2, join five 2⅜" strips of fabric II together end to end. Cut resulting strip in half and join border 2 to quilt top sides, trimming excess.

Finishing

1. Quilt as desired. We stitched in-the-ditch for all of the patchwork, stippled the infield, and made simple rows of lines around the track.

2. Using 2½"-wide strips of fabric II, make 365" of straight-grain binding and bind quilt.

Quilt Assembly

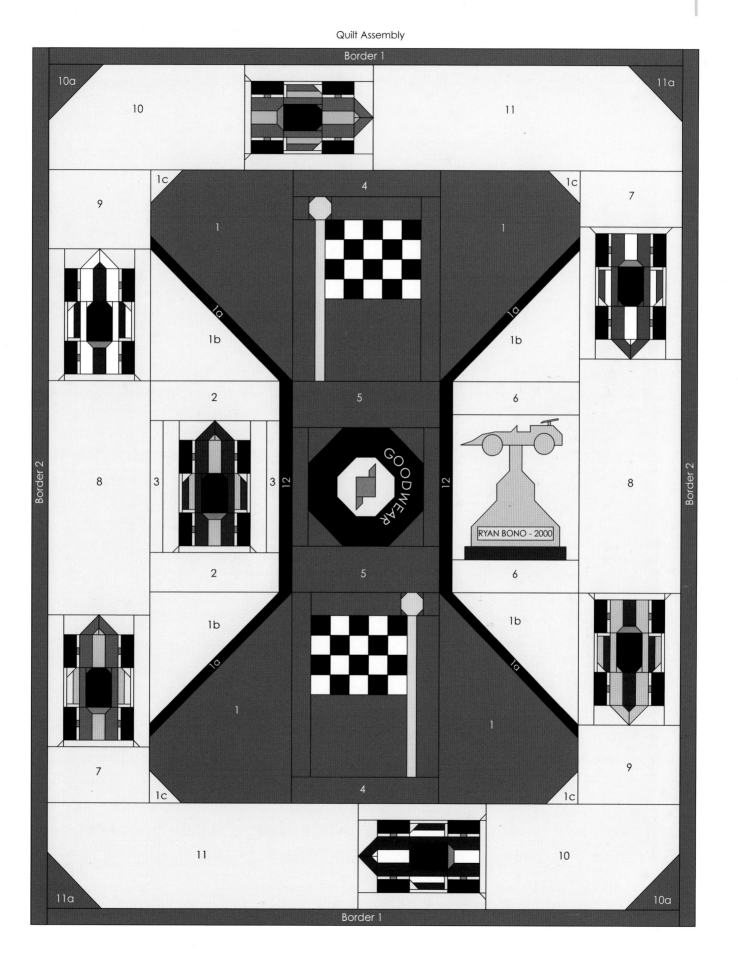

Race Day

Cut 1 for trophy top.
Satin stitch solid lines in black.

That's My Baby

FABRIC
TIPS Warm colors contrast with the cool blues to give the illusion of fuzzy white polar bears basking in the sunlight while they are seated in the pleasing cold of their environment. A frosty print background makes the scene even cooler. Warm and cool colors integrate happily to bring Mom and Baby front and center.

Materials

Fabric I	(peach print)	⅜ yard
Fabric II	(bright orange check)	⅛ yard
Fabric III	(bright orange solid)	¼ yard
Fabric IV	(light blue print)	⅜ yard
Fabric V	(medium blue print)	⅛ yard
Fabric VI	(dark slate print)	⅛ yard
Fabric VII	(dark navy print)	⅜ yard
Fabric VIII	(white-on-muslin print)	½ yard
Fabric IX	(white-on-white print)	¼ yard
Fabric X	(light tan print)	¼ yard
Fabric XI	(bright pink print)	⅛ yard
Backing	(quilt)	1⅛ yard
	(pillow)	1½ yard
Batting		37" x 37"

That's My Baby

35" x 35"
Designed by Dallas and Pam Bono.

Cutting

From Fabric I, cut: (peach print)

- One 8½"-wide strip. From this, cut:
    One - 8½" square (1)
  Cut remainder into two 2½" x 33½" strips. From these, cut:
    One - 2½" x 18¾" (61)
    One - 2½" x 5¾" (21)
    Two - 2½" x 4½" (2)
    Two - 2½" squares (4)
    One - 1½" x 2½" (8)
    Two - 1¾" squares (15a)
    Two - 1½" squares (11a)
    Two - 1¼" squares (11b)
    Two - 1" x 3¾" (10)

From Fabric II, cut: (bright orange check)

- One 2½"-wide strip. From this, cut:
    Five - 2½" x 4½" (6, 7)
    Three - 2½" squares (4a, 5)

From Fabric III, cut: (bright orange solid)

- One 6½"-wide strip. From this, cut:
    One - 6½" square (1a)
  Cut remainder into two 2½" x 35½" strips. From these, cut:
    One - 2½" x 22¼" (63)
    One - 2½" x 19¼" (22)
    One - 2½" x 3½" (64)
    Seven - 2½" squares (3, 6a)

From Fabric IV, cut: (light blue print)

- One 8½"-wide strip. From this, cut:
    One - 8½" square (1b)
  Cut remainder into one 4¼" x 33½" strip, and one 2½" x 33½" strip.

- From the 4¼"-wide strip, cut:
    One - 4¼" x 11¾" (23)
    One - 1¾" x 4¼" (37)
    One - 1½" x 4¼" (41)
    One - 3¼" x 4½" (12)
    One - 2¾" x 11½" (24)

- From the 2½"-wide strip, cut:
    Two - 2½" squares (14a, 25a)
    One - 1½" x 2½" (9)
    One - 2¼" x 4½" (17)
    One - 1¾" x 2¼" (44)
    One - 1¾" square (47b)
    One - 1½" square (18a)
    Two - 1¼" squares (11c)

From Fabric V, cut: (medium blue print)

- One 3½"-wide strip. From this, cut:
    One - 3½" x 8½" (19)
    One - 2½" square (35a)
    One - 2¼" square (45)

From Fabric VI, cut: (dark slate print)

- One 2¾" wide strip. From this, cut:
    One - 2¾" x 11½" (36)
    One - 2¾" x 8½" (20)
    One - 2¼" square (46)
    One - 1¾" x 2¼" (47a)

From Fabric VII, cut: (dark navy print)

- One 3½"-wide strip. From this, cut:
    One - 3½" x 24" (65)
    One - 1¾" x 3½" (70)
    One - 1" x 3½" (58)
    One - 2¼" x 3¼" (69)
    One - 2¾" x 3" (49)
    One - 2½" x 4" (62)
    Two - 1¾" squares (66a)

- Three 1¾"-wide strips. From these, cut:
    One - 1¾" x 35½" (72)
    One - 1¾" x 34¼" (71)
    One - 1¾" x 27¼" (60)
    One - 1½" x 4¾" (67)
    Two - 1¼" squares (50a, 68b)
    One - 1" square (68a)

From Fabric VIII, cut: (white-on-muslin print)

- One 6½"-wide strip. From this, cut:
    One - 6½" x 10½" (15)
    Two - 6½" x 7½" (51)
    One - 1¼" x 5¼" (48)
    Two - 2½" x 4¾" (14, 66)
    One - 1¾" x 4¾" (47)
    Two - 3¾" x 4" (11)

- One 4½"-wide strip. From this, cut:
    Two - 4½" x 11¾" (25, 35)
    Two - 2" x 4½" (13, 16)
    Two - 1½" x 4½" (42)
    Two - 1¾" x 4¼" (39)
    One - 2½" x 3¾" (18)

- One 3½"-wide strip. From this, cut:
    One - 3½" x 11" (26)
    Two - 3" x 3¾" (33)
    One - 1¾" x 3¼" (68)
    Two - 1½" x 3" (42b)
    One - 1¾" x 2¾" (50)
    Two - 2½" squares (27a)
    Two - 1¾" squares (28a)
    One - 1½" square (19a)
    Three - 1" squares (47c, 59d)

From Fabric IX, cut: (white-on-white print)

- One 4"-wide strip. From this, cut:
    One - 4" x 9" (53)
    One - 3" x 3½" (30)
    One - 2½" x 3½" (54)
    Two - 1¾" x 3¼" (52)
    One - 3" x 4½" (34)
    Two - 2½" x 3" (29)
    Two - 2¾" squares (55a)
    One - 1¾" x 6½" (40)

- One 1½"-wide strip. From this, cut:
    One - 1½" x 9" (43)
    One - 1½" x 5½" (32)
    Two - 1" x 1½" (56a)
    Two - 1" x 1¾" (33a)
    Six - 1" squares (33b, 39a, 59e)

From Fabric X, cut: (light tan print)

- One 3"-wide strip. From this, cut:
    Two - 3" squares (25b, 35b)
    Two - 2¾" x 3" (24a, 36a)
    Two - 2¼" x 3" (57)
    One - 2¾" x 11" (27)
    Two - 2¾" x 3½" (55)
    Two - 2½" squares (51a)

- One 2¼"-wide strip. From this, cut:
    Two - 2¼" x 4" (28)
    Four - 1" x 2" (59a, 59c)
    Two - 1¾" x 5¼" (38)
    Two - 1¾" x 2½" (52a)
    Two - 1½" x 3¼" (42a)
    Four - 1½" squares (31, 42c)

- One 1¼"-wide strip. From this, cut:
    Four - 1¼" squares (29a)
    Two - 1¼" x 1¾" (33a)
    Two - 1" x 1¾" (56)
    Two - 1" x 4½" (58a)
    Six - 1" squares (29b, 30a, 42d)

From Fabric XI, cut: (bright pink print)
    Four - 1" x 1½" (59, 59b)
    Bear ears and paw pads

From scraps of solid tan and solid black, cut noses and eyes.

Assembly

Units for Sections A and B

1. For section A, use diagonal corner technique on page 8 to make one of unit 1.

2. Use diagonal corner technique to make two each of units 4 and 6. To make unit 4, place 2½" squares of fabrics I and II right sides together, stitching diagonally down center. Trim seam and press.

3. For section B, use diagonal corner technique to make one each of units 14, 15, 18, and 19.

4. Use diagonal corner technique to make two each of unit 11, referring frequently to illustration for placement of mirror-image diagonal corner units.

Sections A and B

1. Refer to block A assembly diagram and begin by joining units 2, 3, and 4 in a horizontal row as shown. Join this row to top of unit 1.

2. Join units 3, 2, 3, and 4 in a vertical row as shown. Join this row to left side of section A, matching seams.

3. Join units 5, 6 and 7 in a horizontal row as shown. Add this row to top of section A.

4. Join units 7, 6, and 7 in a vertical row and join to left side of section A to complete section A.

5. To piece section B, refer to section B assembly diagram below, and begin by joining units 8 and 9. Join units 10 and 11. Join combined units 10-11 to right side of combined units 8-9 as shown.

6. Join units 12 and 13, then add unit 14 to bottom of combined units. Join all combined units on left side of section in a row as illustrated, then add unit 15 to right side.

7. Join units 16 and 17. Join combined units 10-18 in a vertical row.

8. Join units 19 and 20, then add unit 21 to top of combined units as shown and add to right side of combined units 10-18. Join units 8-15 and units 10-20 together; then add unit 22 to top to complete section B.

Units for Section C

1. Use diagonal corner technique to make one each of units 25, 27, 30, and 35.

2. Use diagonal corner technique to make two each of units 28, 29 and 33, keeping in mind that they are mirror-image units, and referring frequently to illustrations. To make mirror-image unit 33, refer to illustration, and join 1" x 1¾" strips of fabric IX with 1¼" x 1¾" strips of fabric X. Place these strip sets (33a) as shown in illustration, and join as you would for any diagonal corner.

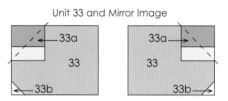

Unit 33 and Mirror Image

3. Use diagonal corner technique on page 9 to make one each of units 24 and 36.

Section C

1. To piece section C, refer to assembly diagram for section C and begin by joining units 23, 24, and 25 in a row as shown.

2. Join units 26 and 27.

Section A

Section B

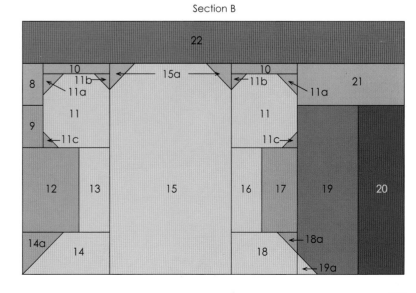

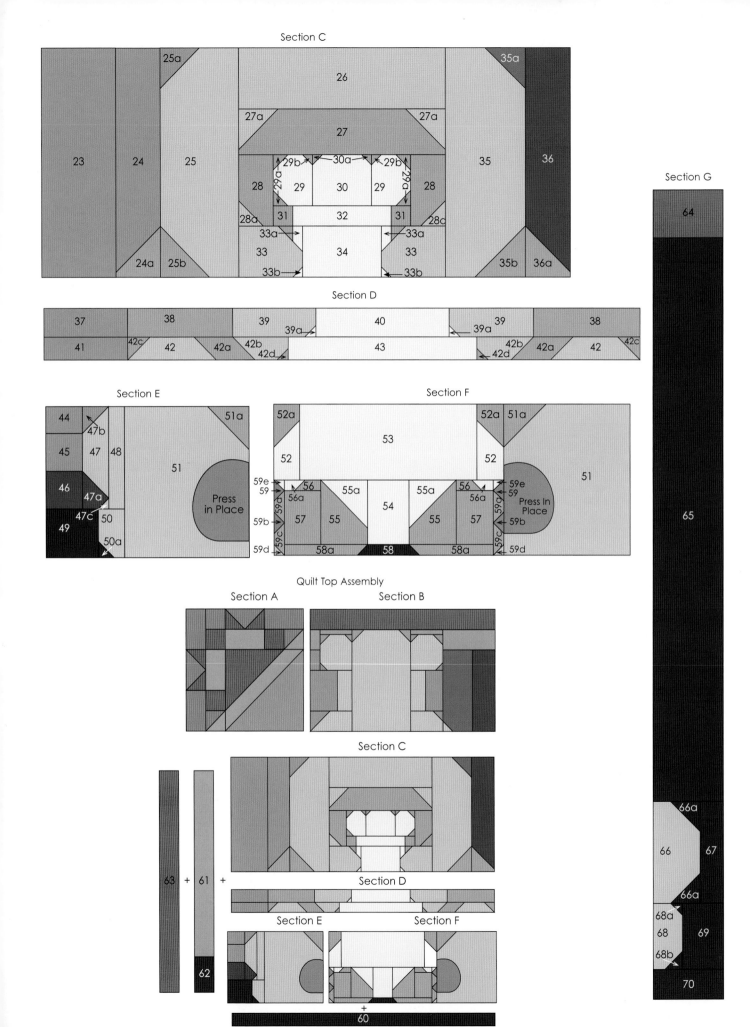

Section C

Section D

Section E

Section F

Section G

Quilt Top Assembly

Section A

Section B

Section C

Section D

Section E

Section F

3. Join units 29, 30, 29 in a horizontal row. Join units 31, 32, and 31 in a horizontal row and combine these two rows, then join unit 28 to opposite ends, placing mirror-image units correctly.

4. Join mirror image units 33 to opposite ends of unit 34. Join these units to bottom of center section, and combined units 26-27 to top.

5. Join units 35 and 36.

6. Referring to the assembly diagram, join all units to complete section C.

Units for Section D

1. Use diagonal corner technique (page 8) to make two of mirror image unit 39.

2. Use diagonal end technique (page 10) to make two of mirror unit 42. Refer to the illustation below for construction of unit 42. Add diagonal corners after diagonal end construction is completed.

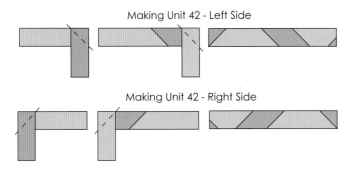

Making Unit 42 - Left Side

Making Unit 42 - Right Side

Section D

Referring to the illustration, join units in two horizontal rows as shown. Join the two rows to complete section D.

Units for Section E

1. Use diagonal corner technique to make one each of units 50 and 51.

2. Use diagonal end technique to make one of unit 47. Make diagonal end, then add diagonal corners 47b and c.

Section E

1. Join units 44, 45, and 46 in a vertical row. Join units 47 and 48, then join the two rows together.

2. Join units 49 and 50 and add to combined units. Before joining unit 51, cut and press Mom's large paw pad appliqué (page 94) in place on unit 51 so that straight edge of her paw pad is sewn in seam to eliminate raw edge. Join unit 51 to right side to complete section E.

Units for Section F

1. Use diagonal corner technique to make one of unit 51. Press paw pad appliqué in place on mirror-image unit 51 as for section E.

2. Use diagonal corner technique to make two of mirror-image units 55.

3. Use diagonal end technique to make one of unit 58.

4. Use diagonal end technique to make two each of mirror image units 52, 56, and 59. Unit 59 is a continuous diagonal end (same as unit 42, shown on the left). Make diagonal ends first, then add diagonal corners 59d and 59e.

Section F

1. Join mirror-image units 52 to opposite ends of unit 53 as shown. Join both units 56 and 57, referring to illustration of section F for correct placement of mirror images.

2. Join combined units 54-57 together in a horizontal row, join unit 58 to bottom of these combined units, matching seams, then add mirror-image units 59 to opposite ends. Then join to bottom of combined units 52-53-52.

3. Join unit 51 to right side to complete section F.

Units for Section G

Use diagonal corner technique to make one each of units 66 and 68.

Section G

To piece section G, refer to the illustration and begin by joining units 66 and 67. Join units 68 and 69. Join all units in a long vertical row as shown to complete section G.

Top Assembly

1. Join sections A and B. Join sections E and F, then join unit 60 to bottom of combined E and F sections.

2. Join sections C, D, and E-F.

3. Join units 61 and 62, then add unit 63 to left side of these combined units. Add to left side of combined sections.

4. Join combined A-B sections to top, then add section G to right side.

5. To complete block, join unit 71 across top of block, then add unit 72 to left side.

That's My Baby

Embellishment

1. Refer to instructions on Baby's arm below, and trace Baby's arms onto Baby's body with water-erasable pen.

2. Thick lines show areas where we have satin stitched to make Mom and Baby stand out. For Mom's head bottom, draw a 45° angle line 4½" down from top of shoulder on each side of head as shown. Connect ends of these diagonal lines with 3" long straight line as shown. Referring to block illustration on right, repeat this procedure for Baby's head bottom, drawing a 45° angle line from corner of seam at Mom's paw, 1½" down. Repeat for both sides and connect diagonal lines with a straight line. Draw chins and mouths on mom and baby.

3. Trace and cut all appliqué pieces as directed on patterns on page 94. Press all appliqués in place, referring to block illustration at top for correct placement.

4. Set your sewing machine on close, medium-wide satin stitch, and use medium-tan thread to satin stitch chin and head lines on both bears. Use tan to stitch Baby's arms and outline of Baby's head, body and feet. Use the tan for Mom's arms.

5. Please note that when you stitch around Baby's body and Mom's arms, you will be using seam lines as your guide. Satin stitch along these seam lines. Use black thread for mouths and coordinating thread for all other appliqués. Highlights in both eyes are worked with white thread, either by machine or hand embroidery.

6. See cover photograph for optional color choices and instructions for completing pillow and wall quilt.

Pillow Back

Embellishment Lines

Baby's Arm

Trace arm with dot at top of rear haunch seam as shown on illustration. Repeat for right side, turning pattern over for mirror image.

Finishing Pillow

1. Cut two backing pieces for pillow each 35½" wide and 25" long. For each backing piece, press under ½", and then another ½" along one 35½" side as shown. Topstitch hem in place. Lay each backing piece, right sides together along raw edges of pillow top. Backing pieces should overlap 7". Baste in place.

2. If you want to include cording and tassels, baste cording between top and backing along edges of right side of pillow top, clipping at corners. Ends of cording should tuck under so cording overlaps and has a nice finish with no raw edges. Add tassels by pinning them in corners, tassels facing inwards. Baste all in place. Pin backing as directed in step 1 and stitch around outside edges. Turn right side out and insert 35" pillow form.

Finishing Wall Quilt

(See alternative color scheme below.)

1. Cut 37" squares of backing and batting. Sandwich batting between backing and top, and baste the three layers together. Work in satin stitch through all three layers using coordinating thread to match backing for your bobbin thread.

2. Quilt remainder as desired. Cut four 3"-wide strips of fabric VII and join together end to end for continuous french fold binding. Make a hanging sleeve if desired and sew into top seam when binding. Make a bow from fabric VII, and pin it under Baby's chin.

That's My Baby

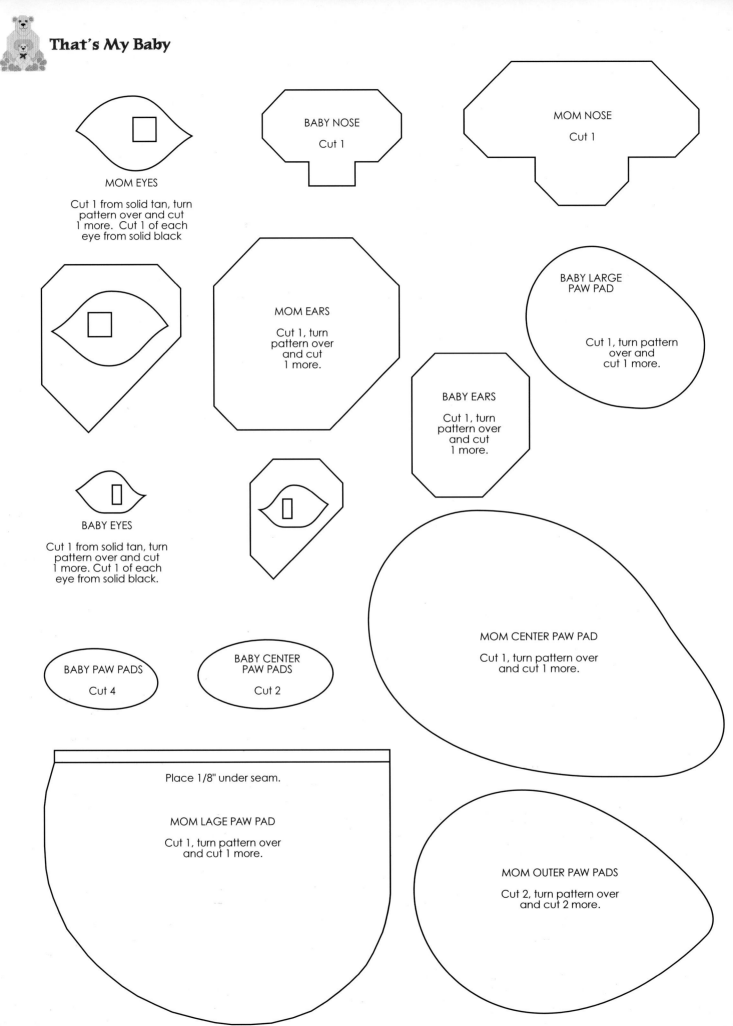

MOM EYES

Cut 1 from solid tan, turn
pattern over and cut
1 more. Cut 1 of each
eye from solid black

BABY NOSE

Cut 1

MOM NOSE

Cut 1

BABY LARGE
PAW PAD

Cut 1, turn pattern
over and
cut 1 more.

MOM EARS

Cut 1, turn
pattern over
and cut
1 more.

BABY EARS

Cut 1, turn
pattern over
and cut
1 more.

BABY EYES

Cut 1 from solid tan, turn
pattern over and cut
1 more. Cut 1 of each
eye from solid black.

MOM CENTER PAW PAD

Cut 1, turn pattern over
and cut 1 more.

BABY PAW PADS

Cut 4

BABY CENTER
PAW PADS

Cut 2

Place 1/8" under seam.

MOM LAGE PAW PAD

Cut 1, turn pattern over
and cut 1 more.

MOM OUTER PAW PADS

Cut 2, turn pattern over
and cut 2 more.

Materials

Fabric I	(light pink print)	1⅜ yards
Fabric II	(dark pink batik)	⅜ yard
Fabric III	(green print)	⅝ yard
Fabric IV	(dark gold print)	¼ yard
Fabric V	(metallic gold print)	¼ yard
Fabric VI	(light gold print)	¼ yard
Fabric VII	(pale gold print)	¼ yard
Fabric VIII	(pale yellow solid)	½ yard
Fabric IX	(bright yellow print)	½ yard
Fabric X	(solid dark purple)	½ yard
Fabric XI	(dark purple print)	⅜ yard
Fabric XII	(dark magenta batik)	½ yard
Fabric XIII	(dark blue print)	⅜ yard
Fabric XIV	(light blue print)	⅝ yard
Fabric XV	(ivory print)	½ yard
Backing		3¾ yards
Batting		66" x 72"
Appliqué film		1½ yards
Tear-away stabilizer		1¼ yards
Gold metallic thread		

The Stuff Dreams Are Made Of

59¾" x 66"
Designed by Pam Bono and Mindy Kettner.
Quilted by Wanda Nelson.

This design creates a mystical illusion of a royal world, which we kept in mind when selecting fabrics. The pink cloud fabric gives a misty feeling, as does the green for the rainbow. We chose a metallic gold print for the stars and carried the metallic look into the appliqué. We used appropriate texture prints for the star's rays and the three tower roofs. Our purple print had a nice light and dark texture, but still gave a strong accent. The dark magenta on the path and two towers is a batik, which enhances a mystical feeling while adding the necessary depth of dramatic color. The door frame and wall behind the door are lighter shades, allowing the dark, solid purple door to stand out and catch your eye as the entrance to this magical castle in the stars.

Cutting

From Fabric I, cut; (pink print)

- One 13¾"-wide strip. From this, cut:
    - One - 3½" x 13¾" (31)
    - One - 11½" x 13½" (29)
    - One - 8" x 13½" (59)
    - One - 7½" x 13" (30)
    - One - 6¼" x 12¾" (20)
    - One - 4" x 11½" (14)

- One 8¾"-wide strip. From this, cut:
    - One - 8¾" x 9¼" (52)
    - One - 8" x 8¾" (60)
    - One - 8"x 15¾" (58)
    - One - 7⅛" sq. (15) cut in half diagonally to yield two triangles.

- One 7½" wide strip. From this, cut:
    - One - 7½" sq. (21c)
    - One - 6¼" x 7¼" (1)
    - One - 6¾" x 10¾" (61)
    - One - 6¾" x 10¼" (61f)
    - One - 3" x 6¾" (28)
    - One - 2¼" x 6¼" (8)

- One 6¾"-wide strip. From this, cut:
    - One - 6¾" x 9¼" (51)
    - One - 5¾" x 6½" (27)
    - One - 5" x 6½" (7)
    - One - 5¾" x 9¾" (40)
    - One - 4¼" x 5¾" (33)
    - One - 2½" x 5¾" (50a)
    - One - 5" x 5¼" (12)

- One 5"-wide strip. From this, cut:
    - One - 5" square (41a)
    - One - 4" x 11¼" (13)
    - One - 3½" square (4a)
    - One - 2½" x 3½" (5)
    - One - 1½" x 3½" (32)
    - One - 2¾" square (57c)
    - One - 2½" x 2¾" (10)
    - Two - 2½" squares (9c, 53a)

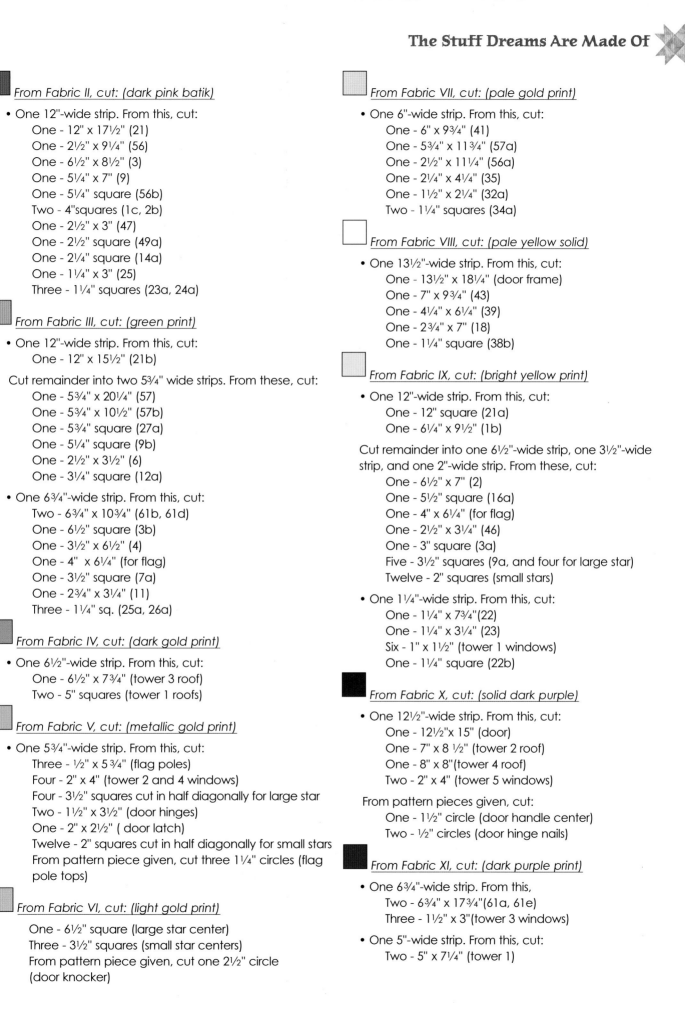

From Fabric II, cut: (dark pink batik)

- One 12"-wide strip. From this, cut:
    One - 12" x 17½" (21)
    One - 2½" x 9¼" (56)
    One - 6½" x 8½" (3)
    One - 5¼" x 7" (9)
    One - 5¼" square (56b)
    Two - 4"squares (1c, 2b)
    One - 2½" x 3" (47)
    One - 2½" square (49a)
    One - 2¼" square (14a)
    One - 1¼" x 3" (25)
    Three - 1¼" squares (23a, 24a)

From Fabric III, cut: (green print)

- One 12"-wide strip. From this, cut:
    One - 12" x 15½" (21b)

Cut remainder into two 5¾" wide strips. From these, cut:
    One - 5¾" x 20¼" (57)
    One - 5¾" x 10½" (57b)
    One - 5¾" square (27a)
    One - 5¼" square (9b)
    One - 2½" x 3½" (6)
    One - 3¼" square (12a)

- One 6¾"-wide strip. From this, cut:
    Two - 6¾" x 10¾" (61b, 61d)
    One - 6½" square (3b)
    One - 3½" x 6½" (4)
    One - 4" x 6¼" (for flag)
    One - 3½" square (7a)
    One - 2¾" x 3¼" (11)
    Three - 1¼" sq. (25a, 26a)

From Fabric IV, cut: (dark gold print)

- One 6½"-wide strip. From this, cut:
    One - 6½" x 7¾" (tower 3 roof)
    Two - 5" squares (tower 1 roofs)

From Fabric V, cut: (metallic gold print)

- One 5¾"-wide strip. From this, cut:
    Three - ½" x 5¾" (flag poles)
    Four - 2" x 4" (tower 2 and 4 windows)
    Four - 3½" squares cut in half diagonally for large star
    Two - 1½" x 3½" (door hinges)
    One - 2" x 2½" (door latch)
    Twelve - 2" squares cut in half diagonally for small stars
    From pattern piece given, cut three 1¼" circles (flag pole tops)

From Fabric VI, cut: (light gold print)

    One - 6½" square (large star center)
    Three - 3½" squares (small star centers)
    From pattern piece given, cut one 2½" circle (door knocker)

From Fabric VII, cut: (pale gold print)

- One 6"-wide strip. From this, cut:
    One - 6" x 9¾" (41)
    One - 5¾" x 11¾" (57a)
    One - 2½" x 11¼" (56a)
    One - 2¼" x 4¼" (35)
    One - 1½" x 2¼" (32a)
    Two - 1¼" squares (34a)

From Fabric VIII, cut: (pale yellow solid)

- One 13½"-wide strip. From this, cut:
    One - 13½" x 18¼" (door frame)
    One - 7" x 9¾" (43)
    One - 4¼" x 6¼" (39)
    One - 2¾" x 7" (18)
    One - 1¼" square (38b)

From Fabric IX, cut: (bright yellow print)

- One 12"-wide strip. From this, cut:
    One - 12" square (21a)
    One - 6¼" x 9½" (1b)

Cut remainder into one 6½"-wide strip, one 3½"-wide strip, and one 2"-wide strip. From these, cut:
    One - 6½" x 7" (2)
    One - 5½" square (16a)
    One - 4" x 6¼" (for flag)
    One - 2½" x 3¼" (46)
    One - 3" square (3a)
    Five - 3½" squares (9a, and four for large star)
    Twelve - 2" squares (small stars)

- One 1¼"-wide strip. From this, cut:
    One - 1¼" x 7¾" (22)
    One - 1¼" x 3¼" (23)
    Six - 1" x 1½" (tower 1 windows)
    One - 1¼" square (22b)

From Fabric X, cut: (solid dark purple)

- One 12½"-wide strip. From this, cut:
    One - 12½" x 15" (door)
    One - 7" x 8½" (tower 2 roof)
    One - 8" x 8" (tower 4 roof)
    Two - 2" x 4" (tower 5 windows)

From pattern pieces given, cut:
    One - 1½" circle (door handle center)
    Two - ½" circles (door hinge nails)

From Fabric XI, cut: (dark purple print)

- One 6¾"-wide strip. From this,
    Two - 6¾" x 17¾" (61a, 61e)
    Three - 1½" x 3" (tower 3 windows)

- One 5"-wide strip. From this, cut:
    Two - 5" x 7¼" (tower 1)

■ *From Fabric XII, cut: (dark magenta batik)*

- One 13½"-wide strip. From this, cut:
  - One - 8½" x 13½" (44)
  - One - 7½" x 9¾" (42)
  - One - 6¾" x 22" (61c)
  - One - 2¾" x 4¼" (37)
  - Three - 1¼" squares (36a, 38a)

■ *From Fabric XIII, cut: (dark blue print)*

- One 9½"-wide strip. From this, cut:
  - One - 9½" x 10½" (16)
  - One - 6¼" x 9¼" (1a)
  - One - 4½" square (2a)
  - One - 4" x 6¼" (for flag)
  - One - 2" x 2¾" (19)
  - One - 1½" x 2¾" (17)
  - Three - 2" x 4"(tower 6 windows)

▨ *From Fabric XIV, cut: (light blue print)*

- One 18"-strip. From this, cut:
  - One - 18" x 21¾"(54)

☐ *From Fabric XV, cut: (ivory print)*

- One 11½"-wide strip. From this, cut:
  - One - 11½" x 18"(53)
  - One - 11½" x 14½" (49)

Cut remainder into one 3½"-wide strip and two-3¼"
wide strips. From these, cut:
  - Two - 2½" x 3½" (45)
  - Two - 1¼" x 3½" (22a, 24)
  - One - 2½" x 3¼" (48)
  - One - 1¼" x 3¼"(26)
  - One - 2¾" square (54b)

- One 4¼"-wide strip. From this, cut:
  - One - 4¼" x 18" (55)
  - Three - 3¼" x 4¼"
    (34, 36, 38)
  - One - 2½" x 6" (50)
  - One - 2½" square (54a)

Assembly

Section A

1. To prepare section A for assembly,
   begin by trimming the corners from
   units 8, 12, 13, 14, 28, 29, 30, and
   31 as shown in castle diagram
   on page 100. Measure
   each corner according
   to the measurement
   shown for that
   unit and trim.

2. Use diagonal corner technique on page 8 to make one
   each of units 2, 3, 4, 7, 12, 14, 16, 23, 24, 25, 26, and 27.

3. Referring to unit 1 diagram, use diagonal end
   technique to join 1, 1a, and 1b; then add
   diagonal corner 1c. Trim corners as shown. Draw
   a line from 1a to the corner. Add ¼" for seam
   allowance and trim. Unit 15 triangle is not added
   until later. Set it aside.

Unit 1

Trim along
dashed line

4. Using diagonal end technique (page 10) make
   units 9, 21, and 22; then add diagonal corners
   after the rest of the unit is completed.

5. To assemble section A, begin by joining units 5 and 6, then
   join units 2, 3, 4, 5-6, 7, and 8 in a horizontal row as shown.

6. Join units 10 and 11, then join units 9, 10-11, 12,
   and 13 in a row. Join this row to the top of the
   row made in step 5, matching seams, then
   add unit 14 to top of this section as shown.
   After adding unit 14, join unit 15 triangle to unit
   1 as shown. Triangle will extend beyond the
   top of unit 1 as shown in illustration. Add unit 1
   to left side of combined rows, matching rainbow seams.

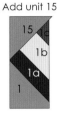

Add unit 15

7. Join units 17, 18, and 19 in a horizontal row, then add
   unit 16 to top of this row as shown. Join units 22-26 as
   shown, then add unit 21 to top of this row, matching
   seams carefully.

8. Join unit 28 to top left side of unit 27 as illustrated. Add
   these combined units to combined units 21-26. Join unit 20
   to left side of combined units 16-19, then add these units to
   combined units 21-28 as shown. Join this completed
   section to top section.

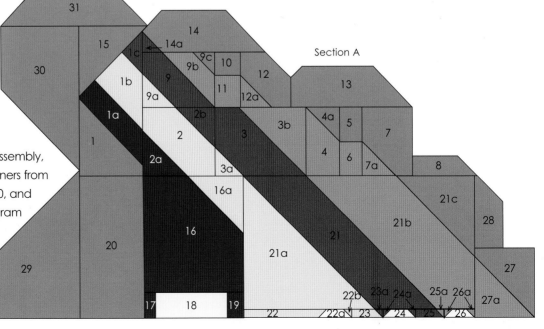

Section A

9. Join trimmed unit 29 to left side of section A, matching raw edges at bottom of units 20 and 29. Press out. Join unit 30 to top of section, matching raw edges at top of trimmed unit 30 and unit 1. Add unit 31 to top as shown to complete section A.

Section B

1. Prepare section B for assembly; begin by trimming the corners from units 33, 40, 51 and 52 as shown in castle diagram of on page 100. Measure and trim as in section A, step 1.

2. Use diagonal corner technique to make one each of units 34, 36, 38, 41, 49, 53, and 54.

3. Use diagonal end technique to make one each of units 32, 50, 56, and 57. To make combined units 55-56, refer to illustration. Complete diagonal end unit 56, then join units 55 and 56 as shown. Add diagonal corner 56b. For unit 57, add diagonal corner 57c after diagonal ends are assembled.

4. To assemble section B, begin by joining units 32, 33, 34, 35, 36, 37, 38, and 39 in a horizontal row. Join units 40, 41, 42, and 43 in a horizontal row. Join the two rows together, matching seams as shown, then add unit 44 to right side.

5. Join units 45, 46, 47 and 48 in a horizontal row. Join unit 49 to bottom of this row, then add resulting row to other combined units as shown.

6. Join units 50 and 51, then add unit 52 to bottom of these combined units. Join units 53, 54, and 55-56 in a row as shown. Add combined units 50-52 to left side as shown. Join top and bottom sections together, carefully matching seams, then add unit 57 to right side.

7. Referring to diagram, join sections A and B, matching all seams where necessary.

Section C

1. Trim corners from units 58, 59, and 60 as in sections A and B, step 1. Join together in a vertical row as shown.

2. Join section C to right side of green rainbow and clouds as shown on page 100.

Section D

1. Section D is a continuous diagonal end with units 61 and 61f trimmed after the entire unit is assembled.

2. Join section D to bottom of castle as shown, matching seams to complete castle.

Section C

Section D

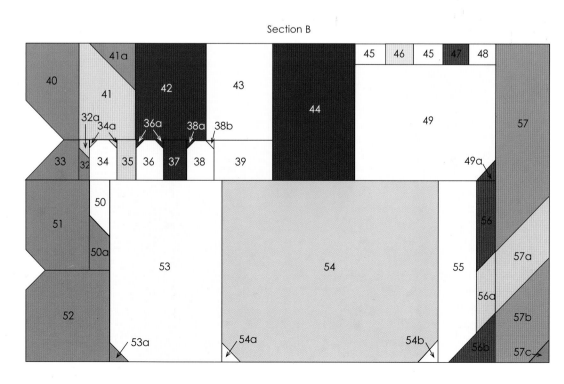

Section B

Units 55-56

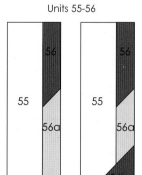

Stars

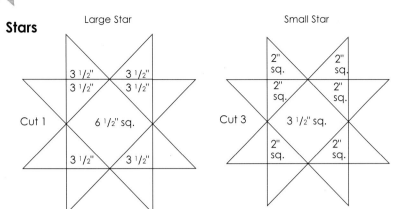

Large Star

Small Star

Cut 1

6 ½" sq.

3 ½" 3 ½"
3 ½" 3 ½"
3 ½" 3 ½"

Cut 3

3 ½" sq.

2" sq. 2" sq.
2" sq. 2" sq.
2" sq. 2" sq.

Stars

1. To make large star, use diagonal corner technique to add the 3½" squares of fabric IX to the 6½" star center. Add diagonal corners one at a time, trim seam and press out, then add other corners in order. For star points, cut 3½" squares of fabric V in half diagonally to yield eight triangles. Join triangles to star and press out.

2. Make each small star in the same manner, adding the 2" squares of fabric IX to the 3½" star center and using 2" squares of fabric V for points. Make three.

Diagram of Units and Corner Trimming

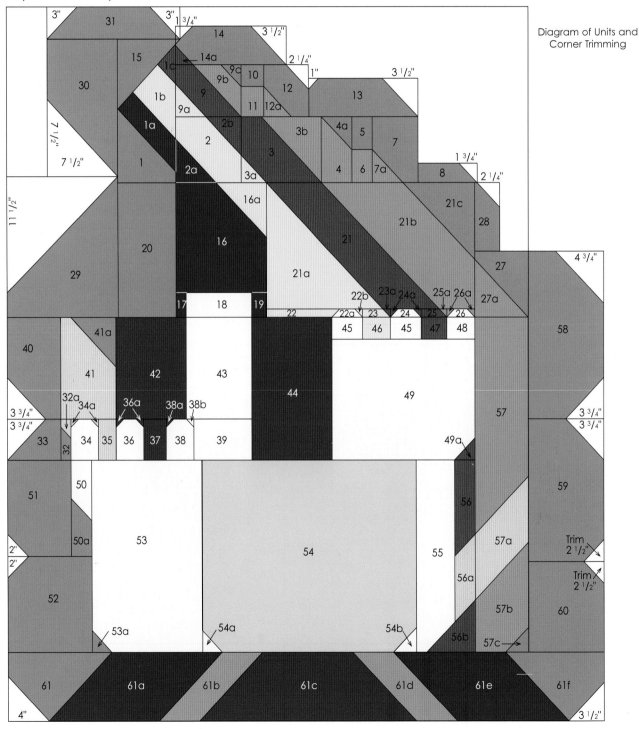

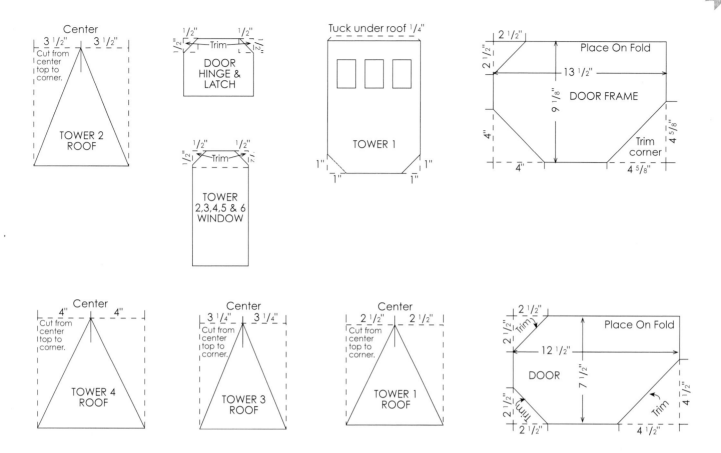

Other Appliqué Units

1. Refer to illustrations of door frame and door. Follow cutting instructions given on each illustration. Cut these pieces and set aside.

2. All appliqué pieces that must be cut from squares or rectangles are illustrated. Follow instructions on each illustration for correct cutting procedure for each piece. Note that all windows require that you trim ½" from each top corner as shown.

3. Patterns are given for the flags, door knocker, flagpole tops, and door hinge nails. Cut each out as directed.

Appliqué

• Refer to the photo for appliqué placement.

• Please note that we placed tear-away stabilizer behind our appliqués.

• Appliqué pieces should be in place before you draw clouds and thin 8-point stars as shown.

• All appliqué pieces are cut out rather than drawn on appliqué film (see Robert's Special Appliqué Technique, page 11).

1. Lay each piece in place and press according to the manufacturer's instructions, fusing the appliqués to the quilt top. For the flags, you will want to place the flag itself first; then lay the flagpole in place so it covers the raw edge of the flag. Add the circular flagpole top and press in place. The roofs will be fused last.

2. For the door, center the door frame first and fuse in place. Center the door on top of the door frame and press in place, then add the hinges, latch, and door knocker.

3. After all appliqué pieces (including stars) have been fused in place, mark lines shown on the door and circular cloud shapes with a water-erasable pen. Add the thin 8-point stars as well.

4. We were very liberal with the use of gold metallic thread, and used it for the entire appliqué in the clouds, on the door and on tower 2 and 4 windows. We used a wide satin stitch around the four appliqué stars and a medium-wide stitch around the other appliqués. A thinner stitch was used for the circular shapes in the clouds and the thin stars.

5. Use coordinating thread to appliqué the remainder of the pieces.

Finishing

1. Quilt as desired.

2. Make 5 yards of 2½"-wide bias binding and bind.

Appliqué Placement

Cut 1 from
fabric V

DOOR HANDLE
CENTER

Cut 1 from
fabric X

DOOR KNOCKER

Tower 2

Tower 3

Tower 4

Tower 5

Tower 1

Tower 1

Tower 6

Door

FLAG

Cut 1 from fabric III
Cut 1 from fabric XIII
Cut 1 from fabric IX

FLAG POLE TOP

Cut 3 from
fabric IV

DOOR HINGE NAILS

Cut 2 from
fabric X

Touchdown

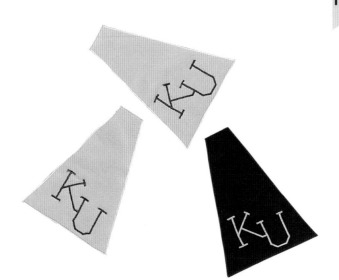

The football field is in basic browns and greens with bright white for the yardlines. This simplicity of solid basics allows you to use your own school colors on the helmets and megaphones, along with school letters. If you can acquire a school patch, what better place for it than the helmet?

FABRIC TIPS

Cutting

From Fabric I, cut: (solid green)

- Six 5"-wide strips. From these, cut:
    - Four - 5" x 38" (11)
    - Two - 2¾" x 5" (1)
    - Six - 5" x 9½" (12)
    - Two - 5" x 5¾" (3)

- Five 3½"-wide strips. From these, cut:
    - Nine - 3½" x 12½" (8, 17)
    - One - 3½" x 8¾" (15)
    - Nineteen - 3½" squares (7a, 14a)

- Two 2¾"-wide strips. From these, cut:
    - Two - 2¾" x 17" (18)
    - One - 2¾" x 12½" (16)
    - Four - 2" x 8" (5)

- Three 2"-wide strips. From these, cut:
    - Eight - 2" x 12½" (6, 9)

From Fabric II, cut: (solid white)

- Eight 2½"-wide strips for straight-grain binding

- Twenty-three 2"-wide strips. From these, cut:
    - Two - 2" x 41" (21)
    - Six - 2" x 38" (10)
    - Four - 2" x 9½" (13)
    - Six - 2" x 29½" pieced for (26)
    - Four - 2" x 34¼" pieced for (20)
    - Four 2" x 32" pieced for (25)
    - Two - 2" x 17" (19)

From Fabric III, cut: (solid camel)

- Five 11¾"-wide strips. From these, cut:
    - Four - 11¾" x 42½" pieced for (24)
    - One - 11¾" x 41" (23)

- One 2¾"-wide strip. From these, cut:
    - One - 2¾" x 41" (22)

From Fabric IV, cut: (solid light tan)

- Two 2"-wide strips. From these, cut:
    - Four - 2" x 9½" (4)
    - Two - 2" x 5" (2)
    - Four - 1½" x 6" (7b)

Materials

Fabric I	(solid green wool)	1¾ yards
Fabric II	(solid white wool)	2 yards
Fabric III	(solid camel wool)	1⅞ yards
Fabric IV	(solid light tan wool)	⅛ yard
Fabric V	(solid gold wool or school color)	⅝ yard
Fabric VI	(solid navy wool or school color)	⅝ yard
Fabric VII	(solid brown wool)	½ yard
Fabric VIII	(solid black wool)	scrap
Appliqué film		2 yards
Tear-away stabilizer		2 yards
Backing		5½ yards
Batting		72" x 83"

Touchdown

66" x 87"
Designed by Pam Bono
and Mindy Kettner.
Quilted by Faye Gooden.

From Fabric V, cut: (solid gold or school color)

- One 9½"-wide strip. From this, cut:
  One - 9½" x 11¾" (14)
  Five - 6⅛" x 8¼" (cut as shown for megaphones)
- One 8¼"-wide strip. From this, cut:
  Six - 6⅛" x 8¼" (megaphones)
  One - 3½" square (14b)

From Fabric VI, cut: (solid navy or school color)

- Two 8¼"-wide strips. From these, cut:
  Ten - 6⅛" x 8¼" (cut as shown for megaphones)
  One - 4" x 6½" (for face guard)
Use remainder for school letters that fit on helmet.

From Fabric VII, cut: (solid brown)

- One 12½"-wide strip. From this, cut:
  Four - 6½" x 12½" (7)

From Fabric VIII, cut: (solid black)

Cut one 1" circle for face guard

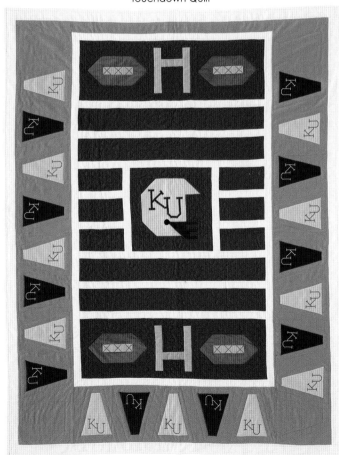

Touchdown Quilt

Assembly

Goal Posts and Footballs

1. For goal posts, refer to illustration of quilt and begin by joining units 1, 2, and 3 in a vertical row. Add units 4 to opposite sides, then add units 5 to top and bottom. Join units 6 to sides as shown. Make two.

2. For footballs, use diagonal corner technique to join units 7a to each corner as shown. Make four. Use appliqué film according to manufacturer's directions and the Techniques section (page 11) and press it to back of each unit 7b. Center unit 7b on football as shown and press in place. Draw X's on unit 7b as shown, using a water-erasable pen. Place tear-away stabilizer behind unit 7b and satin stitch in place with coordinating thread. Satin stitch X's with brown thread.

3. Join units 8 to top and bottom of each football. Referring to quilt diagram, join units 9 to one side of each football. Join footballs to opposite ends of goal posts as shown for top and bottom of quilt.

Helmet and Grass

1. You can use your own school colors for helmet, face guard, and megaphones. Begin helmet construction by using diagonal corner technique to join units 14a. Place one green 3½" square on top of a helmet-colored 3½" square. Stitch from corner to corner diagonally for unit 14b. Trim seam and press. Join unit 14b to unit 15, then add combined units to helmet. Join unit 16 to top of helmet and unit 17 to bottom. Join units 18 to opposite sides of helmet, then add unit 19 as shown.

2. Draw the face guard and circle patterns on appliqué film as directed (page 106). Press these to the back of appropriate fabric. Cut out face guard and circle. Press on helmet and grass area as shown, and satin stitch around the appliqué pieces.

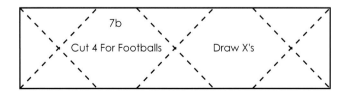

7b
Cut 4 For Footballs   Draw X's

3. Copying from a lettering book or your own school logo, draw school letters on appliqué film and press to helmet. Satin stitch around letters.

4. Join units 12 and 13 as shown. Make two of these sections and join to opposite sides of units 19.

5. Referring to quilt illustration, join three of unit 10 with two of unit 11 as shown. Make two. Join these combined units to top and bottom of helmet section, then add goal post and football sections as shown.

6. Join two unit 20 pieces together end to end. Find the center of quilt and mark with a pin. With right sides together, place seam of unit 20 over pin so that center of border and quilt are matched. Join border to sides of quilt. Join units 21 to top and bottom of quilt.

Sidelines and Megaphones

1. Join unit 22 to top of quilt. Using our drawing of the megaphone as a guide, cut a plastic template for megaphone. Draw twenty-one megaphones on appliqué film, positioned as in diagram A. Press appliqué film to back of megaphone fabrics. Cut out twenty-one megaphones.

2. At this time, you may wish to letter the megaphones with your school letters, using a chalk marker or soapstone for the darker fabric and a blue water-erasable pen for the lighter fabric.

3. Referring to quilt diagram, place megaphones so that there is 1¾" of sideline fabric above and below megaphones. Begin with sideline unit 23. Place outer megaphones 1¾" from each end as shown, then fill in remainder of megaphones 4½" apart. Press in place and place tear-away stabilizer behind each megaphone. With coordinating thread, satin stitch around all megaphones on this unit. At this time you may want to satin stitch your lettering as well as shown in illustration. When this is completed, join unit 23 to bottom of quilt.

4. For sideline units 24, once again refer to illustration, and press first megaphone 10" from edges as shown, spacing remainder 4½" apart. Stitch megaphones as you did for unit 23, then join both units 24 to opposite sides of quilt.

5. Join units 25 to top and bottom of quilt. Join three 2" x 29½" sections of unit 26 together end to end. Join resulting strips to sides of quilt, trimming excess.

6. Quilt as desired and bind with 312" of straight-grain binding.

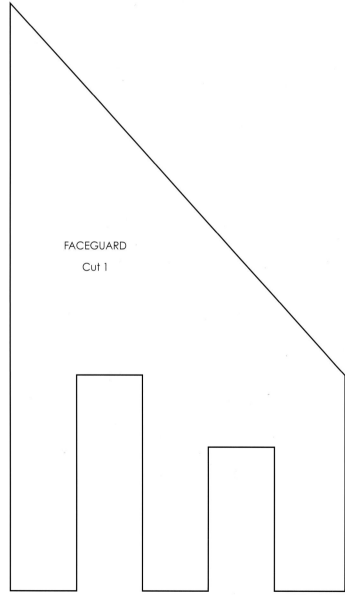

FACEGUARD

Cut 1

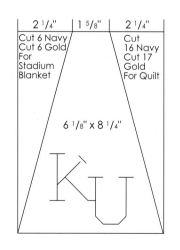

2 1/4"	1 5/8"	2 1/4"
Cut 6 Navy Cut 6 Gold For Stadium Blanket		Cut 16 Navy Cut 17 Gold For Quilt

6 1/8" x 8 1/4"

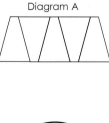

Diagram A

Cut 1 black for faceguard

Quilt Assembly

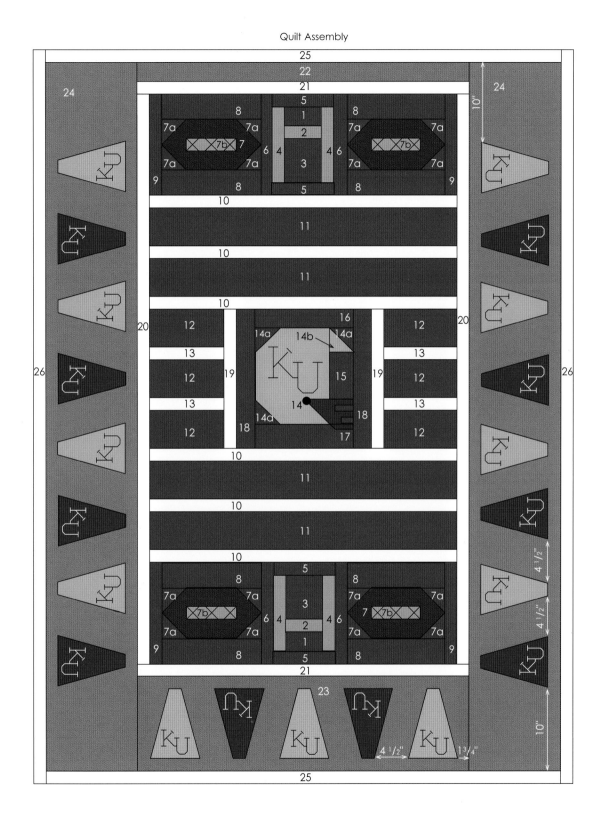

◆ Touchdown Stadium Blanket

Materials

■ Fabric I	(solid green wool)	⅜ yard
□ Fabric II	(solid white wool)	¾ yard
▨ Fabric III	(solid camel wool)	1 yard
▦ Fabric IV	(solid gold wool or school color)	½ yard
▨ Fabric V	(solid navy wool or school color)	½ yard
■ Fabric VI	(solid black wool)	scrap
	Appliqué film	1½ yards
	Tear-away stabilizer	1½ yards
	Backing	2 yards

Cutting

▨ *From Fabric I, cut: (solid green)*

- One 3½"-wide strip. From this, cut:
  One - 3½" x 12½" (4)
  One - 3½" x 8¾" (2)
  Three - 3½" squares (1a, 1b)
- Two 2¾"-wide strips. From these, cut:
  Two - 2¾" x 17" (5)
  One - 2¾" x 12½" (3)

□ *From Fabric II, cut: (solid white)*

- Five 2½"-wide strips for straight-grain binding
- Six 2"-wide strips. From these, cut:
  Two - 2" x 41" (10)
  Four - 2" x 22¼" pieced to make (11)
  Two - 2" x 20" (7)
  Two - 2" x 17" (6)

▨ *From Fabric III, cut: (solid camel)*

- Three 11"-wide strips. From these, cut:
  Two - 11" x 41" (9)
  Two - 11" x 20" (8)

▦ *From Fabric IV, cut: (solid gold or school color)*

- One 9½"-wide strip. From this, cut:
  One - 9½" x 11¾" (1)
  Four - 6⅛" x 8¼" (megaphones)
- One 6⅛"-wide strip. From this, cut:
  Two - 6⅛" x 8¼" (megaphones)
  One - 3½" square (1b)

▨ *From Fabric V, cut: (solid navy or school color)*

- One 8¼"-wide strip. From this, cut:
  Six - 6⅛" x 8¼" (megaphones)

- One 4"-wide strip. From this, cut:
  One - 4" x 6½" (face guard)

■ *From Fabric VI, cut: (solid black)*

Cut one 1" circle for face guard

Assembly

Helmet and Grass

1. Use your school colors for helmet, face guard, and megaphones. Begin helmet construction by using diagonal corner technique to make units 1a. Place one green 3½" square on top of helmet-colored 3½" square. Stitch from corner to corner diagonally for unit 1b. Trim seam and press. Join unit 1b to unit 2, then add combined unit to helmet. Join unit 3 to top of helmet, and unit 4 to bottom. Join units 5 to opposite sides of helmet, then add units 6 and 7 as shown.

2. Draw faceguard and circle pattern (page 106) on appliqué film as directed. Press to the back of appropriate fabric. Cut out faceguard and circle. Press these to helmet and grass area as shown, and satin stitch around the appliqué pieces.

3. Copying from a lettering book or your own school logo, draw the school letters on appliqué film and press them to helmet. Satin stitch around letters.

Sidelines and Megaphones

1. Using our drawing (page 106) of the megaphone as a guide, cut a plastic template for megaphone. Draw twelve megaphones on appliqué film, butted up together by opposite ends (see diagram A, page 106). Press appliqué film to back of megaphone fabrics. Cut out all megaphones.

2. At this time, you may wish to letter the megaphones with your school letters, using a chalk marker or soapstone for the darker fabric and a blue water-erasable pen for the lighter fabric.

3. Referring to stadium blanket photograph, place megaphones so that there is 1⅜" of sideline fabric above and below megaphones. Begin with sideline units 8. Place outer megaphones 1¾" from each end as shown, then fill in remainder of megaphones 2¼" apart. Press in place and place tear-away stabilizer behind each megaphone. Satin stitch around all megaphones on this unit using coordinating thread. At this time you may want to satin stitch your lettering as well as shown in photograph. When this is completed, join unit 8 to top and bottom of blanket.

4. For sideline units 9, once again refer to photo, and press first megaphone 10¾" from edges as shown, spacing remainder 3⅜" apart. Stitch megaphones as you did for unit 8, then join both units 9 to opposite sides of stadium blanket.

5. Join units 10 to top and bottom of blanket. Join two 2" x 22¼" sections of unit 11 together end to end. Join resulting strip to sides of blanket, trimming excess.

6. Quilt as desired and bind with 180" of straight-grain binding.

Touchdown Stadium Blanket

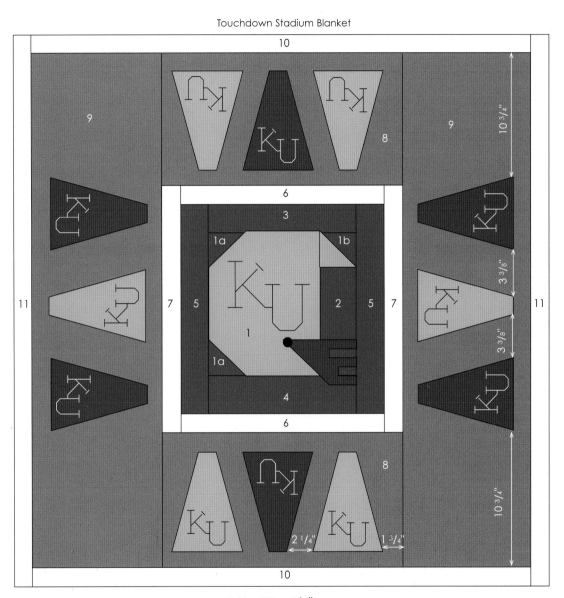

Finished Size: 43½" square

Bibliography

Anderson, Alex. *Hand Quilting with Alex Anderson*. Lafayette: C&T Publishing, 1998.

_____ . *Rotary Cutting with Alex Anderson*. Lafayette: C&T Publishing, 1999.

_____ . *Start Quilting with Alex Anderson*. Lafayette: C&T Publishing, 1997.

Hargrave, Harriet. *Heirloom Machine Quilting, 3rd Edition*. Lafayette: C&T Publishing, 1995.

_____ . *Mastering Machine Appliqué*. Lafayette: C&T Publishing, 1991.

Johnson-Srebro, Nancy. *Measure the Possibilities*. Lafayette: C&T Publishing, 1999.

McClun, Diana and Nownes, Laura. *Quilts, Quilts, and More Quilts!*. Lafayette: C&T Publishing, 1995.

Sienkiewicz, Elly. *Appliqué 12 Easy Ways!* Lafayette: C&T Publishing, 1991.

Index

About the Author

After twenty years in the quilting business, Pam Bono has learned to follow her own drummer. Pam's husband Robert takes an active part in helping with both sewing and designing. With this book, Pam has collaborated with friends and family members to create quilts for children of all ages. Their fresh approach and innovatiave concepts have quilters all over the country excited about these new designs.

Pam Bono Designs's products: patterns, two books with Oxmoor House, The Angler™, and The Angler 2™ have been well-received in the quilt world and have been featured internationally in top magazines in the United States, Australia, New Zealand, and the United Kingdom.

Pam has appeared on television and travels nationwide teaching classes, giving seminars, and being the featured artist at quilt shows.

C&T Booklist

An Amish Adventure: 2nd Edition, Roberta Horton

Anatomy of a Doll: The Fabric Sculptor's Handbook, Susanna Oroyan

Appliqué 12 Easy Ways! : Charming Quilts, Giftable Projects & Timeless Techniques, Elly Sienkiewicz

Art & Inspirations: Ruth B. McDowell, Ruth B. McDowell

The Art of Silk Ribbon Embroidery, Judith Baker Montano

The Art of Classic Quiltmaking, Harriet Hargrave and Sharyn Craig

The Artful Ribbon, Candace Kling

At Home with Patrick Lose: Colorful Quilted Projects, Patrick Lose

Baltimore Beauties and Beyond (Volume I), Elly Sienkiewicz

Basic Seminole Patchwork, Cheryl Greider Bradkin

The Best of Baltimore Beauties, Elly Sienkiewicz

Beyond the Horizon: Small Landscape Appliqué, Valerie Hearder

Color From the Heart: Seven Great Ways to Make Quilts with Colors You Love, Gai Perry

Crazy Quilt Handbook, Judith Montano

Crazy with Cotton, Diana Leone

Curves in Motion: Quilt Designs & Techniques, Judy B. Dales

Deidre Scherer: Work in Fabric & Thread, Deidre Scherer

Designing the Doll: From Concept to Construction, Susanna Oroyan

Easy Pieces: Creative Color Play with Two Simple Blocks, Margaret Miller

Elegant Stitches: An Illustrated Stitch Guide & Source Book of Inspiration, Judith Baker Montano

Everything Flowers: Quilts from the Garden, Jean and Valori Wells

Exploring Machine Trapunto: New Dimensions, Hari Walner

Fabric Shopping with Alex Anderson, Seven Project to Help You: Make, Successful Choices, Build Your Confidence, Add to Your Fabric Stash, Alex Anderson

Faces & Places: Images in Appliqué, Charlotte Warr Andersen

Fancy Appliqué: 12 Lessons to Enhance Your Skills, Elly Sienkiewicz

Fantastic Fabric Folding: Innovative Quilting Projects, Rebecca Wat

Fantastic Figures: Ideas & Techniques Using the New Clays, Susanna Oroyan

Focus on Features: Life-like Portrayals in Appliqué, Charlotte Warr Andersen

Forever Yours: Wedding Quilts, Clothing & Keepsakes, Amy Barickman

Freddy's House: Brilliant Color in Quilts, Freddy Moran

Free Stuff for Collectors on the Internet, Judy Heim and Gloria Hansen

Free Stuff for Crafty Kids on the Internet, Judy Heim and Gloria Hansen

Free Stuff for Gardeners on the Internet, Judy Heim and Gloria Hansen

Free Stuff for Quilters on the Internet, 2nd Ed. Judy Heim and Gloria Hansen

Free Stuff for Sewing Fanatics on the Internet, Judy Heim and Gloria Hansen

Free Stuff for Stitchers on the Internet, Judy Heim and Gloria Hansen

From Fiber to Fabric: The Essential Guide to Quiltmaking Textiles, Harriet Hargrave

Hand Quilting with Alex Anderson: Six Projects for Hand Quilters, Alex Anderson

Heirloom Machine Quilting, Third Edition, Harriet Hargrave

Imagery on Fabric, Second Edition, Jean Ray Laury

Impressionist Palette, Gai Perry

Impressionist Quilts, Gai Perry

Jacobean Rhapsodies: Composing with 28 Appliqué Designs, Patricia B. Campbell and Mimi Ayars

Judith Baker Montano: Art & Inspirations, Judith Baker Montano

Kaleidoscopes: Wonders of Wonder, Cozy Baker

Kaleidoscopes & Quilts, Paula Nadelstern

Make Any Block Any Size, Joen Wolfrom

Mariner's Compass Quilts, New Directions, Judy Mathieson

Mastering Machine Appliqué, Harriet Hargrave

Mastering Quilt Marking: Marking Tools & Techniques, Choosing Stencils, Matching Borders & Corners, Pepper Cory

Michael James: Art & Inspirations, Michael James

The New England Quilt Museum Quilts: Featuring the Story of the Mill Girls. With Instructions for 5 Heirloom Quilts, Jennifer Gilbert

The New Sampler Quilt, Diana Leone

On the Surface: Thread Embellishment & Fabric Manipulation, Wendy Hill

Patchwork Persuasion: Fascinating Quilts from Traditional Designs, Joen Wolfrom

Patchwork Quilts Made Easy, Jean Wells (co-published with Rodale Press, Inc.)

The Photo Transfer Handbook: Snap It, Print It, Stitch It!, Jean Ray Laury

Pieced Clothing Variations, Yvonne Porcella

Pieced Flowers, Ruth B. McDowell

Pieced Roman Shades: Turn Your Favorite Quilt Patterns into Window Hangings, Terrell Sundermann

Pieces of an American Quilt, Patty McCormick

Piecing: Expanding the Basics, Ruth B. McDowell

Plaids & Stripes: The Use of Directional Fabrics in Quilts, Roberta Horton

Quilts for Fabric Lovers, Alex Anderson

Quilts from Europe, Projects and Inspiration, Gül Laporte

Quilts from the Civil War: Nine Projects, Historical Notes, Diary Entries, Barbara Brackman

Quilts, Quilts, and More Quilts! Diana McClun and Laura Nownes

Recollections, Judith Baker Montano

RIVA: If Ya Wanna Look Good Honey, Your Feet Gotta Hurt…,Ruth Reynolds

Rotary Cutting with Alex Anderson: Tips, Techniques, and Projects, Alex Anderson

Rx for Quilters: Stitcher-Friendly Advice for Every Body, Susan Delaney Mech, M.D.

Say It with Quilts, Diana McClun and Laura Nownes

Scrap Quilts: The Art of Making Do, Roberta Horton

Shadow Quilts: Easy to Design Multiple Inage Quilts, Patricia Magaret and Donna Slusser

Simply Stars: Quilts that Sparkle, Alex Anderson

Six Color World: Color, Cloth, Quilts & Wearables, Yvonne Porcella

Skydyes: A Visual Guide to Fabric Painting, Mickey Lawler

Small Scale Quiltmaking: Precision, Proportion, and Detail, Sally Collins

Soft-Edge Piecing, Jinny Beyer

Special Delivery Quilts, Patrick Lose

Start Quilting with Alex Anderson: Six Projects for First-Time Quilters, Alex Anderson

Stripes in Quilts, Mary Mashuta

Through the Garden Gate: Quilters and Their Gardens, Jean and Valori Wells

Tradition with a Twist: Variations on Your Favorite Quilts, Blanche Young and Dalene Young Stone

Trapunto by Machine, Hari Walner

Travels with Peaky and Spike: Doreen Speckmann's Quilting Adventures, Doreen Speckmann

The Visual Dance: Creating Spectacular Quilts, Joen Wolfrom

Wild Birds: Designs for Appliqué & Quilting, Carol Armstrong

Wildflowers: Designs for Appliqué & Quilting, Carol Armstrong

Willowood: Further Adventures in Buttonhole Stitch Appliqué, Jean Wells

Women of Taste: A Collaboration Celebrating Quilt Artists and Chefs, Girls, Inc.

Yvonne Porcella: Art & Inspirations, Yvonne Porcella

For more information write for a free catalog:
C&T Publishing, Inc.
P.O. Box 1456
Lafayette, CA 94549
(800) 284-1114
web: www.ctpub.com
e-mail: ctinfo@ctpub.com

For quilting supplies:
Cotton Patch Mail Order
3405 Hall Lane, Dept. CTB
Lafayette, CA 94549
(800) 835-4418
(925) 283-7883
web: www.quiltusa.com